Editor's Note

When this almanac came together in 2023, the city had obtained several new things: a "rat czar," a long-awaited performing arts venue at the World Trade Center, a curvy, cave-like wing for the American Museum of Natural History, a Yayoi Kusama robot in a Louis Vuitton shop window, and a dose of wildfire smoke from Canada that put New Yorkers in an apocalyptic mood. (Mayor Adams said what everyone was thinking: "What the hell is this?") Not to mention a new logo—a lopsided take on Milton Glaser's "I HEART NY" that misses the "mild undertaste of belligerence" of the original, as the *New Yorker*'s Adam Gopnik put it.

In June 2023, a *Times* headline declared the city "Best for Bird-Watching and Good for Rats, Too: No Place Like New York." True. No other place arguably has such a vast cultural landscape—from opera premieres to esoteric performances like a floating concert in a drainage tunnel to battle-rap showdowns in Staten Island. New York alone has artist Felix Morelo cheekily drawing "good luck" and "bad luck" spots on city sidewalks for pedestrians to navigate around, or through.

Only a fraction of 2024's performances, exhibitions, festivals, and other events could fit onto these pages. But I hope that what is here will delight and surprise you. Keep your eyes and ears open for newly announced events to record here and don't forget to check with each venue, as dates are subject to change. New Yorkers know how to take the birds with the rats, the opera and the smoke, the "good luck" and "bad luck" spots. As Gopnik wrote, "We are renewed more by a snarl than a smile. That's *why* we HEART New York."

The Five-Borough Fashion Forecast: It seems that fashion in 2024 will remain in lockstep with popular culture. Just as Mermaidcore and Barbiecore fascinated TikTokers in 2023, we can expect fantastical aesthetics to emerge in response to new films and television shows—so keep your eye on the latest releases if you want to be au courant! While streaming services find themselves at the nexus of fashion and entertainment, we can expect the latest crazes to be reported on social media platforms, where access and immediacy all but guarantee the proliferation of microtrends. Influencers will likely decide what we'll be wearing next; and with so many voices at play, one thing is for sure: trend cycles will be turning over faster than a New York minute.

Still, street fashion will likely remain more consistent according to each urban locale. The neutral tones and simple silhouettes of "quiet luxury" may be on the rise in certain neighborhoods of Manhattan; however, color and eclecticism will endure as stylistic hallmarks of the outer boroughs. And when it comes to navigating their way through it, city dwellers are faced with an ever-present dilemma: fashion or function? Simultaneously on offer: the practicality of cargo pants and capacious carry-all bags, countered by the novelty of micropurses that can hold little more than a metro card. While digital wallets may mean that on-the-go New Yorkers can move through the city unencumbered, wearable tech is sure to become a greater presence in the fashion sector. The latest gadgets may turn into the season's hottest accessories, and come to rival Rolexes and Birkins as icons of conspicuous consumption. Nevertheless, technological advancement is often met with a renewed interest in handcraft, and the rise of artificial intelligence could instead lead to enthusiasm for bespoke garments and handmade decorative elements.

Sustainability will remain at the forefront of the fashion conversation, with many big brands striving for circular production and small businesses prioritizing upcycling and repurposing. When it comes to secondhand shopping, the cosmopolitan consumer will find no shortage of thrift and consignment stores throughout the city. The abundance of vintage clothing on the resale market reflects a range of coexisting aesthetics from different time periods—allowing New Yorkers to experiment with their wardrobes, selectively participate in trends, and cultivate their personal style.

Jan. 15–21

"Now there may be people who move easily into New York without travail, but most I have talked to about it have had some kind of torture before acceptance."
—John Steinbeck

15 MONDAY

☼ 7:19 AM / 4:53 PM

Martin Luther King Jr. Day

Celebrate Martin Luther King Jr. Day with tributes at the Brooklyn Academy of Music or Harlem's Apollo Theater.

16 TUESDAY

☼ 7:18 AM / 4:54 PM

Guildhall Artists in New York at Carnegie Hall

17 WEDNESDAY

☼ 7:18 AM / 4:55 PM   ◐ 1ST QUARTER

1953: Chevrolet's "Dream Car," a prototype of the Corvette, is introduced at GM's Motorama auto show at the Waldorf-Astoria hotel.

18 THURSDAY

☼ 7:17 AM / 4:56 PM

Opening night of the Winter Show art fair at the Park Avenue Armory

19 FRIDAY

☼ 7:17 AM / 4:57 PM

Aerosmith Peace Out: Farewell Tour with the Black Crows at Madison Square Garden

20 SATURDAY

☼ 7:16 AM / 4:58 PM   ♒ AQUARIUS

Jazz at Lincoln Center presents Max Roach Centennial: The JLCO with Wynton Marsalis (and 19th).

21 SUNDAY

☼ 7:16 AM / 4:59 PM

Last chance to see *Morgan's Bibles: Splendor in Scripture* at the Morgan Library and Museum

Jan. 22–28

"Manhattan Island, at its center, inspires utterly baseless optimism—even in me."
   —Kurt Vonnegut

22 MONDAY

☼ 7:15 AM / 5:01 PM

1908: Katie Mulcahey is cited for breaking the day-old (though soon vetoed) Sullivan Ordinance, which barred women from publicly smoking.

23 TUESDAY

☼ 7:15 AM / 5:02 PM

New York Philharmonic presents *Vertigo* in concert (through Jan. 26).

24 WEDNESDAY

☼ 7:14 AM / 5:03 PM

City Center Encores! performs *Once Upon a Mattress* (through Jan. 28).

25 THURSDAY

☼ 7:13 AM / 5:04 PM

○ FULL MOON

New York City Ballet presents *Wheeldon + Martins + Peck* (and Jan. 27, 28, 31, Feb. 3).

26 FRIDAY

☼ 7:12 AM / 5:05 PM

Jazz at Lincoln Center presents *The Blues with Bobby Rush and Shemekia Copeland* (and 27th).

27 SATURDAY

☼ 7:12 AM / 5:07 PM

International Holocaust Remembrance Day

New York Travel and Adventure Show Javits Center (and 28th)

28 SUNDAY

☼ 7:11 AM / 5:08 PM

Last chance to see *Enchanting Imagination: The Objets d'Art of André Chervin and Carvin French Jewelers* at the New-York Historical Society

FEBRUARY

LUNAR NEW YEAR celebrations—from **parades** down Main Street in Flushing, Queens, and Eighth Avenue in Sunset Park, Brooklyn, to firecrackers at Sara D. Roosevelt Park in Manhattan —shine through the frigid gloom of a dark, cold month, ushering in spring with bright red envelopes, cozy get-togethers with family and friends, dancing, dragons, and **festivals at the Museum of Chinese in America and the Metropolitan Museum of Art.** It may be hard to picture spring when you're surrounded by mounds of dirty snow, stomping your salt-encrusted boots in the dim, slanting sunset while waiting for a crosstown bus, or being pushed up the avenue by a strong gust of wind; however, a **Beatrix Potter exhibition opening at the Morgan Library and Museum,** exploring the artist's connection to the natural world and sure to be full of bunnies and garden vegetables, should help.

PROFESSOR VATICINATE SAYS, *the first ten days of February are damp and freezing, wet and wheezing. Even the Groundhog's shadows shiver and quiver. Midmonth sees the coldest air of the season; these are the days of shivery. A bit of a respite late in the month, but just in time for leap day, a snowy blast from the past.*

NORMALS FOR
CENTRAL PARK

Avg. high: 42.2°
Avg. low: 29.5°
Avg. rainfall: 3.19"
Avg. snowfall: 10.1"

Ninety years ago, on February 9, 1934, the temperature at Central Park plummeted to 15° below zero, the coldest day in NYC weather history. Readings hovered at or below -10° from 3 a.m. to 9 a.m. and did not climb above zero until noon (2°). The high for the day was 7° at 4 p.m. This day also marked the sixty-fourth birthday/anniversary of the U.S. Weather Bureau.

Sky Watch: On the 7th, look to the lower southeast at 6 a.m., when Venus sits to the upper left of a crescent Moon. At 6 p.m., high in the southwest on Valentine's Day, Jupiter is poised at the Moon's upper right. On the 16th, binoculars reveal the Pleiades star cluster to the right of the half Moon.

ANNALS OF THE NIGHT SKY

If you're a New Yorker interested in astronomy, there is an NYC-based astronomy club you might want to join. It's the Amateur Astronomers Association, Inc., organized in 1927 to promote the study of astronomy, emphasizing its cultural and inspirational value. It provides stargazing sessions, free lectures, a podcast, and a monthly magazine. For more info, visit https://aaa.org/.

NYC BOOK OF THE MONTH
Invisible Man by Ralph Ellison (1952)

In one evocative passage from Ellison's surreal novel, the unnamed protagonist wanders through Harlem streets "covered with ice and soot-flecked snow," and encounters an old man selling baked yams, a taste from his childhood. "I walked along, munching the yam, just as suddenly overcome by an intense feeling of freedom—simply because I was eating while walking along the street," a familiar feeling for many New Yorkers.

NYC MOVIE OF THE MONTH
Working Girl, directed by Mike Nichols,
starring Melanie Griffith, Harrison Ford,
and Sigourney Weaver (1988)

Tess McGill (Melanie Griffith) swaps big hair and secretarial work for a bouncy '80s bob and the identity, job, and boyfriend (Harrison Ford) of her obnoxious boss (Sigourney Weaver) in this fable of ambition and commuting. The Staten Island Ferry wistfully glides between two worlds. Location photography started February 16, 1988, in the New Brighton neighborhood of Staten Island.

In this leap year, February has 29 days.

● Jan. 29–Feb. 4

"Cats, with their vast resourcefulness, their marvelous urbanity, have been misunderstood in this city. . . . They are instinct with pavements, alleys, and mud gardens, for in a city they are the autochthons."

—*New Yorker*, 1928

29 MONDAY

☼ 7:10 AM / 5:09 PM

1845: Edgar Allan Poe's "The Raven" is published in the *New-York Mirror*.

30 TUESDAY

☼ 7:09 AM / 5:10 PM

Boston Symphony Orchestra at Carnegie Hall (and 29th)

31 WEDNESDAY

☼ 7:08 AM / 5:12 PM

Final opportunity to see *New Frontiers at Top of the Rock* at Rockefeller Center

1 THURSDAY

☼ 7:07 AM / 5:13 PM

The Following Evening at the Perelman Performing Arts Center (through Feb. 18)

2 FRIDAY

☼ 7:06 AM / 5:14 PM ◑ 3RD QUARTER

Groundhog Day

Jazz at Lincoln Center presents Masters of Form: Duke, Jelly Roll, and Mingus (and 3rd).

3 SATURDAY

☼ 7:05 AM / 5:15 PM

Between Two Knees at the Perelman Performing Arts Center (through Feb. 24)

4 SUNDAY

☼ 7:04 AM / 5:17 PM

Last chance to see *Bellini and Giorgione in the House of Taddeo Contarini* at the Frick Madison

Feb. 5–11

"As only New Yorkers know, if you can get through the twilight, you'll live through the night."
  —Dorothy Parker

5 MONDAY
☼ 7:03 AM / 5:18 PM

Naumburg Foundation Concert at Carnegie Hall

6 TUESDAY
☼ 7:02 AM / 5:19 PM

New York City Ballet presents *All Balanchine* (and Feb. 7, 16, 17).

7 WEDNESDAY
☼ 7:01 AM / 5:20 PM

Chamber Music Society of Lincoln Center presents Inside Chamber Music: Britten's String Quartet No. 2 in C Major.

8 THURSDAY
☼ 7:00 AM / 5:22 PM

Valentine's Concert at Carnegie Hall

9 FRIDAY
☼ 6:59 AM / 5:23 PM ● NEW MOON

Good Medicine at the Perelman Performing Arts Center

10 SATURDAY
☼ 6:58 AM / 5:24 PM

Lunar New Year

Squid plays Brooklyn Steel.

11 SUNDAY
☼ 6:57 AM / 5:25 PM

New York City Ballet presents *Copland Dance Episodes: A Ballet by Justin Peck* (and Feb. 13, 17, 21).

Feb. 12–18

"No, New York was not a modern city. For, having been so at the beginning, before any other city, it now on the contrary already had a horror of this."
—Salvador Dalí

12 MONDAY
☼ 6:55 AM / 5:27 PM

Lincoln's Birthday

National Symphony Orchestra at Carnegie Hall

13 TUESDAY
☼ 6:54 AM / 5:28 PM

Santtu-Matias Rouvali conducts Strauss's *An Alpine Symphony* and Bernstein's *Serenade* with the New York Philharmonic (and Feb. 8, 10, 11).

14 WEDNESDAY
☼ 6:53 AM / 5:29 PM

Ash Wednesday · Valentine's Day

Name a cockroach for your loved one at the Bronx Zoo.

15 THURSDAY
☼ 6:52 AM / 5:30 PM

Susan B. Anthony's Birthday

Bruce Liu makes his New York Philharmonic debut performing Rachmaninoff and Dvořák (through Feb. 17).

16 FRIDAY
☼ 6:50 AM / 5:32 PM ◑ 1ST QUARTER

Jazz at Lincoln Center presents Dianne Reeves: Lovestruck (and 17th).

17 SATURDAY
☼ 6:49 AM / 5:33 PM

Jeffrey Osborne plays Sony Hall.

18 SUNDAY
☼ 6:48 AM / 5:34 PM

Last chance to see *Stéphane Mandelbaum* at the Drawing Center

Feb. 19–25

"The fact of its being the chief city of the New World, alone caused it to be the principal magnet of attraction for all the expert criminals of the Old World.'"
—William F. Howe and
  Abraham Hummel, 1886

19 MONDAY

☼ 6:46 AM / 5:35 PM ♓ PISCES

Presidents' Day

Young Steinway Artists at Carnegie Hall

20 TUESDAY

☼ 6:45 AM / 5:35 PM

New York Philharmonic's Lunar New Year Gala

21 WEDNESDAY

☼ 6:44 AM / 5:38 PM

An Evening with John Williams and Yo-Yo Ma at Carnegie Hall

22 THURSDAY

☼ 6:42 AM / 5:39 PM

City Center Encores! presents *Jelly's Last Jam* (Feb. 21–25).

23 FRIDAY

☼ 6:41 AM / 5:40 PM

Beatrix Potter: Drawn to Nature opens at the Morgan Library and Museum.

24 SATURDAY

☼ 6:39 AM / 5:41 PM ○ FULL MOON

Final date to see *Victorian Masterpieces from the Museo de Arte de Ponce, Puerto Rico* at the Metropolitan Museum of Art.

25 SUNDAY

☼ 6:38 AM / 5:42 PM

Last chance to see *We Tried to Warn You! Environmental Crisis Posters, 1970–2020* at Poster House

Feb. 26–Mar. 3

"A quality that permeates the New York air, piercing through the bitterness of February and the languid heat of August . . . the sharp, free, siren quality once defined by Henry James as 'a note of vehemence.'"
—Joan Didion

26 MONDAY

☼ 6:36 AM / 5:43 PM

Metropolitan Opera presents *La Forza del Destino* (through Mar. 29).

27 TUESDAY

☼ 6:35 AM / 5:45 PM

Chamber Music Society of Lincoln Center presents Winter Festival: Calidore String Quartet.

28 WEDNESDAY

☼ 6:33 AM / 5:46 PM

Metropolitan Opera presents *Turandot* (through June 7).

29 THURSDAY

☼ 6:32 AM / 5:47 PM

Outsider Art Fair opens at the Metropolitan Pavilion (through Mar. 3).

1 FRIDAY

☼ 6:30 AM / 5:48 PM

Jazz at Lincoln Center presents Terence Blanchard: A Career Retrospective in Jazz (and 2nd).

2 SATURDAY

☼ 6:29 AM / 5:49 PM

New York Philharmonic's Artist-in-Residence Hilary Hahn performs Bach.

3 SUNDAY

☼ 6:27 AM / 5:50 PM   ◑ 3RD QUARTER

Last chance to see *Nicolas Party and Rosalba Carriera* at the Frick Madison

MARCH

Since the Lunar New Year ushered in spring in February, and Easter comes at the end of March, let's hope this month acquiesces and banishes its usual topsy-turvy weather for some solidly warm, pleasant days. Fifth Avenue's **Easter Parade and Bonnet Festival**—a city tradition since the 1870s, when fashionable parishioners spilled out of Saint Patrick's Cathedral for an afternoon promenade—gives New Yorkers a chance to celebrate by donning enormous hats covered in eggs, flowers, and sometimes even metro cards or Peeps, and their most colorful finery (hopefully not covered by furs or puffer coats). On weekends before the holiday, **Easter egg hunts** can be found all over town from Central and Prospect Parks to the Bronx's Bartow-Pell Mansion, Queens Alley Pond Park, and Staten Island's Walker Park. The Jewish holiday **Purim** gives some New Yorkers another reason to dress up. Celebrated in the orthodox enclaves of Brooklyn, the holiday includes charity, food, and elaborate costumes.

Professor Vaticinate says, *between the 4th and 7th, a nor'easter brings rain up to your craw, followed by a sunny thaw. Later in the month, more unsettled weather. Spring arrives unusually early this year (on the 19th), still, ill winds blow both rain and snow. Sadly, toward month's end, we believe no lamb-like reprieve. Mom may be wearing a wet bonnet in the Easter Parade.*

NORMALS FOR
CENTRAL PARK

Avg. high: 49.9°
Avg. low: 35.8°
Avg. rainfall: 4.29"
Avg. snowfall: 5.0"

Easter's date is determined by the Moon phase. It can come as early as March 22 and as late as April 25. Because of this, the day experiences wide variations in its weather. The coldest Easter was April 1, 1923 (12°). The hottest occurred on April 18, 1976 (96°). Since 1870, measurable snow has occurred only four times on Easter; the greatest amount (4") fell on March 29, 1970. The wettest Easter was April 6, 1958 (2.19" of rain).

SKY WATCH: The Moon makes its closest approach to Earth in 2024 (221,764 miles) on the 10th at 2 a.m. Expect large tides around this date. Spring begins unusually early this year, on the 19th at 11:06 p.m. Spring's first full Moon—the Paschal Moon—falls on the 25th. The following Sunday (the 31st) is Easter; the first one celebrated in March since 2016.

ANNALS OF THE NIGHT SKY

More than three thousand people gathered at the Central Park Mall at 72nd Street on March 7, 1970, to view a 96 percent solar eclipse. The event was cosponsored by the parks department and the Hayden Planetarium. Many, of course, called the planetarium the day before with questions; one person asked if it was selling tickets for the eclipse. "No," was the response, "this particular sky show is being staged by an independent producer."

NYC BOOK OF THE MONTH
A Good Fall: Stories by Ha Jin (2010)

Ha Jin's short story collection depicts the Chinese immigrant experience in and around Flushing, Queens, exploring lives circumscribed by place, money, and the challenges of being caught between two worlds. Complexity builds as the stories progress.

NYC MOVIE OF THE MONTH
Wild Style, directed by Charlie Ahearn, starring Lee Quiñones, Lady Pink, and Fab 5 Freddy (1983)

An artifact of the birth of hip-hop, *Wild Style* premiered at the New Directors/New Films festival in March 1983. The film is full of real-life graffiti, B-boy and hip-hop artists like Busy Bee Starski, the Cold Crush Brothers, Grandmaster Flash, and the Rock Steady Crew, and showcases the interconnected, homegrown art forms that were about to change the world.

March has 31 days.

Mar. 4–10

"Union Square. . . . I really saw people in the air. If you were on the sunny side of the street it was nice, beautiful, but then when you'd hit a corner, you'd get blown away."
—Andy Warhol, 1979

4 MONDAY
☼ 6:26 AM / 5:51 PM

SAVIOUR: A Modern Oratorio
30th Anniversary Performance at Carnegie Hall

5 TUESDAY
☼ 6:24 AM / 5:52 PM

Justin Austin, baritone, Howard Watkins, piano, at Carnegie Hall

6 WEDNESDAY
☼ 6:22 AM / 5:54 PM

Orchestre Métropolitain de Montréal at Carnegie Hall

7 THURSDAY
☼ 6:21 AM / 5:55 PM

Metropolitan Opera presents *Roméo et Juliette* (through Mar. 30).

8 FRIDAY
☼ 6:19 AM / 5:56 PM

International Women's Day

Jazz at Lincoln Center presents Wayne Shorter Celebration (and 9th).

9 SATURDAY
☼ 6:18 AM / 5:57 PM

Flamenco Festival at City Center (Mar. 8–17)

10 SUNDAY
☼ 7:16 AM / 6:58 PM   ● NEW MOON

Daylight saving time begins.

Ramadan begins.

Last chance to see *Something Beautiful: Reframing La Colección* at El Museo del Barrio

Mar. 11–17

"When you're Irish and you don't know a soul in New York and you're walking along Third Avenue . . . there's great comfort in discovering there's hardly a block without an Irish bar."

—Frank McCourt

11 MONDAY

☼ 7:14 AM / 6:59 PM

Like They Do in the Movies at the Perelman Performing Arts Center (Mar. 10–31)

12 TUESDAY

☼ 7:13 AM / 7:00 PM

1963: Cassius Clay recites boxing-themed poetry at the Bitter End on the eve of a fight at Madison Square Garden.

13 WEDNESDAY

☼ 7:11 AM / 7:01 PM

Jaap van Zweden conducts Beethoven, Mendelssohn, and Mozart with the New York Philharmonic (through Mar. 19).

14 THURSDAY

☼ 7:09 AM / 7:02 PM

The Wonder City of the World: Myth-making and the Metropolis opens at Poster House.

15 FRIDAY

☼ 7:08 AM / 7:03 PM

Jazz at Lincoln Center presents Bryan Carter's "Bayard Rustin in Renaissance" (and 16th).

16 SATURDAY

☼ 7:06 AM / 7:04 PM

Rhiannon Giddens plays the Beacon Theatre.

17 SUNDAY

☼ 7:04 AM / 7:05 PM   ◑ 1ST QUARTER

Saint Patrick's Day

Saint Patrick's Day Parade, 5th Ave.

Mar. 18–24

"Harlem is what it is—a new old community waiting for those ambitious people to establish it again."
 —Hilton Als

18 MONDAY

☿ 7:03 AM / 7:06 PM

Last chance to see *Rirkrit Tiravanija: A Lot of People* at MoMA PS1

19 TUESDAY

☿ 7:01 AM / 7:08 PM

Chamber Music Society of Lincoln Center presents An Evening with Michael Stephen Brown.

20 WEDNESDAY

☿ 6:59 AM / 7:09 PM ♈ARIES

Vernal Equinox

Toshiko Takaezu opens at the Noguchi Museum in Queens.

21 THURSDAY

☿ 6:58 AM / 7:10 PM

Max Raabe and Palast Orchestra at Carnegie Hall

22 FRIDAY

☿ 6:56 AM / 7:11 PM

Jazz at Lincoln Center presents Kurt Rosenwinkel (and 23rd).

23 SATURDAY

☿ 6:54 AM / 7:12 PM

Piaf! The Show starring Nathalie Lermitte at the Town Hall.

24 SUNDAY

☿ 6:53 AM / 7:13 PM

Palm Sunday

Purim

Barclays Center hosts March Madness (first and second rounds; and 22nd).

Mar. 25–31

Caught on a side street
in heavy traffic, I said
to the cabbie, I should
have walked. He replied,
"I should have been a doctor."
—Harvey Shapiro

25 MONDAY

☼ 6:51 AM / 7:14 PM   ○ FULL MOON

Curbside composting begins in the
Bronx and Staten Island.

26 TUESDAY

☼ 6:49 AM / 7:15 PM

Metropolitan Opera presents
La Rondine (through Apr. 20).

27 WEDNESDAY

☼ 6:48 AM / 7:16 PM

Standard Time with Michael Feinstein
at Carnegie Hall

28 THURSDAY

☼ 6:46 AM / 7:17 PM

Mahler Chamber Orchestra,
Mitsuko Uchida, piano and director,
at Carnegie Hall

29 FRIDAY

☼ 6:44 AM / 7:18 PM

Good Friday

New York International Auto Show
at Javits Center (through Apr. 7).

30 SATURDAY

☼ 6:43 AM / 7:19 PM

Jazz at Lincoln Center presents
Catherine Russell (and 29th).

31 SUNDAY

☼ 6:41 AM / 7:20 PM

Easter Sunday

Easter Bonnet Parade outside
Saint Patrick's Cathedral

APRIL

THIS IS THE MONTH to finally take your coat to the cleaners, throw open the windows, and dare to expose a shoulder, knee, or bare head. A visit to one of the city's botanical gardens—there are seven throughout the five boroughs, from the Bronx's Wave Hill to Staten Island's Snug Harbor—is the perfect excuse to try out your new spring fashions and snap photos among the blooms. At the **New York Botanical Garden** in the Bronx, you can usually catch the Orchid Show through April, or relish that first sign of spring—the daffodil, which the garden has been cultivating since the early 1900s—with a visit to its famed Daffodil Hill. The city's vest-pocket parks and community gardens come alive, and the **Met's roof garden commission** usually opens this month. Major League Baseball celebrates the date Jackie Robinson broke the color barrier—the perfect time to visit the new **Jackie Robinson Museum** in Lower Manhattan.

PROFESSOR VATICINATE SAYS, *during April's first week, lowery skies spit rain and wet snow in your eye. I hope we're wrong with this forecast, but clouds could eclipse the solar eclipse on the 8th. Midmonth we're treated to a spell of unseasonably warm weather, but later in the month, sunbeams will give way to rain and rising streams. And to finish off April, a rigorous shot of cold takes hold—quite bold!*

NORMALS FOR
CENTRAL PARK
Avg. high: 61.8°
Avg. low: 45.5°
Avg. rainfall: 4.09"
Avg. snowfall: 0.4"

Can a solar eclipse affect the weather? Apparently it did on March 7, 1970, when the Moon covered 96 percent of the Sun for NYC. The temperature at Central Park hit a high that day of 51° at 12:15 p.m. The eclipse began ten minutes later. The temperature then leveled off, and at 1:42 p.m., as the eclipse reached its peak, the mercury dipped to 48°. It rose to 50° after the eclipse ended.

Sky Watch: A slender crescent Moon sits to the upper right of Jupiter on the evening of the 10th and rides between the V-shaped Hyades cluster (to its left) and the Pleiades cluster the following evening (the 11th); a lovely sight in binoculars. The bright blue star Spica sits just below the Moon on the 22nd.

ANNALS OF THE NIGHT SKY

It is rare that a large percentage of the Sun's disk (90 percent) is obscured by the Moon, as will be the case on the 8th. We surveyed all the solar eclipses occurring over NYC between the years 1835 and 2210 and found only eight other instances when an equal or larger amount covered or will cover the Sun. The Big Apple hosted a total eclipse in 1925; two more totals are on the way in 2079 and 2144; and in 2200, the Moon will cover all but 1 percent of the Sun.

NYC BOOK OF THE MONTH
Jazz by Toni Morrison (1992)

The plot of *Jazz*—given away in the first paragraphs—is a violent love triangle, but the heart of the book is an impressionistic, improvisational description of 1920s Harlem and the "City" itself (always capitalized in the book). In spring, Morrison writes, "What can beat bricks warming up to the sun? The return of awnings . . . the darkness under bridges changes from gloom to cooling shade."

NYC MOVIE OF THE MONTH
New Jack City, directed by Mario Van Peebles, starring Wesley Snipes, Ice-T, and Chris Rock (1991)

Village Voice reporter Barry Michael Cooper wrote a screenplay packed with city shots, like a wedding at Grant's Tomb and a hostile encounter on the basketball courts at Saint Nicholas Park on West 135th Street. Location shooting started April 16, 1990. Chris Rock plays the drug addict Pookie, and said that for years after the film premiered, dealers would hug him on the street and slip crack into his pockets.

April has 30 days.

Apr. 1–7

"While some New Yorkers become morose with rain, others . . . say that on rainy days the city's buildings seem somehow cleaner—washed in an opalescence, like a Monet painting."
    —Gay Talese

---

1 MONDAY

☼ 6:39 AM / 7:21 PM   ◑ 3RD QUARTER

April Fool's Day

New York International Music Festival at Carnegie Hall

---

2 TUESDAY

☼ 6:38 AM / 7:22 PM

Camille's Rainbow at Carnegie Hall (through Apr. 6)

---

3 WEDNESDAY

☼ 6:36 AM / 7:23 PM

Nederlands Dans Theater at City Center (through Apr. 6)

---

4 THURSDAY

☼ 6:34 AM / 7:24 PM

Alice Sara Ott performs Ravel's G-major Piano Concerto with the New York Philharmonic (through Apr. 6).

---

5 FRIDAY

☼ 6:33 AM / 7:25 PM

Harmonic Convergence Concert at Carnegie Hall

---

6 SATURDAY

☼ 6:31 AM / 7:26 PM

Lailat al-Qadr

Italian singer Laura Pausini plays The Theater at Madison Square Garden

New York City Tartan Day Parade

---

7 SUNDAY

☼ 6:30 AM / 7:27 PM

Chamber Music Society of Lincoln Center presents *The Soldier's Tale.*

● Apr. 8–14

"Rising above the skyscrapers, the sky surges through the straight streets; it's too vast for the city to tame, and it overflows—it's a mountain sky."
    —Simone de Beauvoir

8 MONDAY

☼ 6:28 AM / 7:28 PM ● NEW MOON

Total solar eclipse occurs from 3:27 PM to 3:35 PM.

Ramadan ends.

Patti LuPone: A Life in Notes at Carnegie Hall

9 TUESDAY

☼ 6:26 AM / 7:29 PM

Eid al-Fitr

2000: The *New Yorker* publishes "One Day—and One Night—in the Kitchen at Les Halles" by Anthony Bourdain.

10 WEDNESDAY

☼ 6:25 AM / 7:30 PM

Metropolitan Opera presents *Fire Shut Up in My Bones* (Apr. 8–May 2).

11 THURSDAY

☼ 6:23 AM / 7:32 PM

Yo-Yo Ma, cello, Kathryn Stott, piano, at Carnegie Hall

12 FRIDAY

☼ 6:22 AM / 7:33 PM

Beatrice Rana performs Rachmaninoff's Piano Concerto No. 2 with the New York Philharmonic (through Apr. 14).

13 SATURDAY

☼ 6:20 AM / 7:34 PM

Ensemble Modern at Carnegie Hall

14 SUNDAY

☼ 6:19 AM / 7:35 PM

Number Our Days: A Photographic Oratorio at the Perelman Performing Arts Center (through Apr. 14)

Apr. 15–21

"New Yorkers are nice about giving you street directions; in fact they seem quite proud of knowing where they are themselves."
—Katharine Brush

15 MONDAY
☼ 6:17 AM / 7:36 PM ◑ 1ST QUARTER

Tax Day

Jackie Robinson Day at MLB

16 TUESDAY
☼ 6:15 AM / 7:37 PM

New York International Music Festival at Carnegie Hall

17 WEDNESDAY
☼ 6:14 AM / 7:38 PM

1951: Mickey Mantle's first game as a New York Yankee, Yankee Stadium

18 THURSDAY
☼ 6:12 AM / 7:39 PM

Olga Neuwirth performs *Project 19* with texts by Emily Dickinson, Walt Whitman, and graffiti artists with the New York Philharmonic (through Apr. 20).

19 FRIDAY
☼ 6:11 AM / 7:40 PM ♉ TAURUS

Jazz at Lincoln Center presents the Sarah Vaughan Centennial (and 20th).

20 SATURDAY
☼ 6:10 AM / 7:41 PM

Spring Family Day at Carnegie Hall

21 SUNDAY
☼ 6:08 AM / 7:42 PM

Lyle Ashton Harris: Our first and last love opens at the Queens Museum.

Apr. 22–28

"Holy the solitude of skyscrapers and pavements! Holy the cafeterias filled with the millions! Holy the mysterious rivers of tears under the streets!"
　　—Allen Ginsberg

22 MONDAY
☼ 6:07 AM / 7:43 PM

Passover begins.

Earth Day

Celebrate Earth Day with a day of service at Queens County Farm.

23 TUESDAY
☼ 6:05 AM / 7:44 PM　○ FULL MOON

John Adams returns to the Metropolitan Opera after ten years for the company premiere of *El Niño* (through May 17).

24 WEDNESDAY
☼ 6:04 AM / 7:45 PM

The New York Philharmonic's Spring Gala

25 THURSDAY
☼ 6:02 AM / 7:46 PM

No Escape: The Legacy of Attica Lives! opens at Poster House.

26 FRIDAY
☼ 6:01 AM / 7:47 PM

Arbor Day

New York City Ballet presents *Masters at Work* (and Apr. 27, 28, May 1, 12).

27 SATURDAY
☼ 6:00 AM / 7:48 PM

Golden Key Music Festival at Carnegie Hall

28 SUNDAY
☼ 5:58 AM / 7:49 PM

NYCRUNS Brooklyn Half Marathon

Apr. 29–May 5

"The trees along this city street
Save for the traffic and the trains
Would make a sound as thin
    and sweet
As trees in country lanes."
    —Edna St. Vincent Millay

29 MONDAY
☼ 5:57 AM / 7:51 PM

New York Pops 41st Birthday Gala at Carnegie Hall

30 TUESDAY
☼ 5:56 AM / 7:52 PM

Passover ends.

Message in a Bottle at City Center (through May 12)

1 WEDNESDAY
☼ 5:55 AM / 7:53 PM   ☽ 3RD QUARTER

Sheku Kanneh-Mason performs Shostakovich's Cello Concerto No. 1 with the New York Philharmonic (through May 4).

2 THURSDAY
☼ 5:53 AM / 7:54 PM

Bavarian Radio Symphony Orchestra at Carnegie Hall

3 FRIDAY
☼ 5:52 AM / 7:55 PM

Jazz at Lincoln Center presents Duke Ellington at 125 (and 4th).

4 SATURDAY
☼ 5:51 AM / 7:56 PM

Go on a Jane's Walk with the Municipal Arts Society in honor of urbanist Jane Jacobs's (1916–2006) birthday.

5 SUNDAY
☼ 5:50 AM / 7:57 PM

Orthodox Easter Sunday

Cinco de Mayo

TD Five Boro Bike Tour

MAY

New Yorkers have astrophysicist and native New Yorker Neil deGrasse Tyson to blame—er, thank—for popularizing one of the city's most Instagrammable events: **Manhattanhenge**. Twice a year in May and July, the setting sun perfectly aligns with Manhattan's cross streets, flooding 14th, 23rd, 34th, 42nd, and 57th Streets with a golden-hour glow as spectators jockey for the best camera angle, oblivious to the chance of getting hit by a car. Other Instagrammable moments in May include catching society's fashionable doyennes gathering for the **"Hat Lunch"** (the Central Park Conservancy's Women's Committee Frederick Law Olmsted Awards Luncheon) around Fifth Avenue and 103rd Street, or capturing a skyline view of Lower Manhattan from the Verrazzano Bridge during the **Five Boro Bike Tour**. For a more sophisticated take on photography, don't miss **MoMA's survey of the work of activist-photographer LaToya Ruby Frazier**.

Professor Vaticinate says, *May gets off to a showery and thundery start; amidst flower blossoms, the Sun plays 'possum. Unsettled and even stormy weather could persist almost to midmonth; skies are scoured by showers. Finally! From the 16th through the 23rd, seven wondrous days we say: warm and clear; enjoy a cold beer. Wouldn't you know it, however: showers and chillier air arrive to put a damper on the holiday weather.*

Normals for Central Park	On May 26, 1979, a game between the New York Mets and the Pittsburgh Pirates ended in a 3–3 tie in the 11th inning because the contest was *fogged out*—a first for Shea Stadium. The game was called by the umpires after a fly ball was lost in the thick fog. Said Joe Torre, the manager of the Mets, "It's an act of God, the fog; you can't argue with that. It's a higher power than ours."
Avg. high: 71.4°	
Avg. low: 55.0°	
Avg. rainfall: 3.96"	

Sky Watch: During the first ten days of May, at 9 p.m., bid a fond adieu to the brightest of all stars, blue-white Sirius, situated just above the west-southwest horizon. One hour before sunrise on the 4th, look above the east-southeast horizon for the waning crescent Moon; well above and to its right is yellow-white Saturn.

ANNALS OF THE NIGHT SKY

The largest object currently circling Earth is the International Space Station (ISS). It's also the brightest, sometimes shining as much as Venus. For its scheduled visit over your neighborhood, go to https://spotthestation.nasa.gov/.

NYC BOOK OF THE MONTH
Washington Square by Henry James (1880)

James's classic novel of thwarted love—about a dashing, but poor, man who wants to marry a rich, but plain, woman, whose father is dead set against the match—captures the manners, anxieties, and cruelty of upper-class New York in settings from a "little parlor" in a "neat little house of red brick" in a middle-class neighborhood on Second Avenue, where the poor man's sister lives, to a stuffy Washington Square drawing room.

NYC MOVIE OF THE MONTH
Speedy, directed by Ted Wilde, starring Harold Lloyd, Ann Christy, and Bert Woodruff (1928)

This silent comedy, about saving the city's last horse-drawn streetcar, features an extended cameo by Babe Ruth (followed by a shorter one by teammate Lou Gehrig) as a terrified passenger in a taxi driven by a baseball fanatic (Harold Lloyd). The madcap ride careens through a series of near misses of automobiles and pedestrians, with Lloyd more interested in his passenger than the road.

May has 31 days.

May 6–12

"New York is full of people on this kind of leave of absence, of people with a feeling for the tangential adventure, the risk venture, the interlude that's not likely to end in any double-ring ceremony."
—Joan Didion

6 MONDAY

☼ 5:49 AM / 7:58 PM

Metropolitan Opera presents *The Hours* (May 5–31).

7 TUESDAY

☼ 5:47 AM / 7:59 PM ● NEW MOON

Royal Conservatory Orchestra with Peter Oundjian and Stewart Goodyear at Carnegie Hall

8 WEDNESDAY

☼ 5:46 AM / 8:00 PM

New York City Ballet presents *Classic NYCB II* (and May 9, 11, 18, 26).

9 THURSDAY

☼ 5:45 AM / 8:01 PM

Ascension Day

Orchestra of Saint Luke's at Carnegie Hall

10 FRIDAY

☼ 5:44 AM / 8:02 PM

Kwamé Ryan conducts world premieres by Melinda Wagner and Mary Kouyoumdjian with the New York Philharmonic.

11 SATURDAY

☼ 5:43 AM / 8:03 PM

Musical Explorers Family Concert at Carnegie Hall

12 SUNDAY

☼ 5:42 AM / 8:04 PM

Mother's Day

LaToya Ruby Frazier: Monuments of Solidarity opens at MoMA.

May 13–19

"As Brooklynites, we can get stung by something, but it's not going to swell and bleed."
—Jacqueline Woodson

13 MONDAY

☼ 5:41 AM / 8:05 PM

An American Soldier at Perelman Performing Arts Center (May 12–19)

14 TUESDAY

☼ 5:40 AM / 8:06 PM

New York City Ballet presents *Contemporary Choreography I* (and May 18, 22, 25).

15 WEDNESDAY

☼ 5:39 AM / 8:07 PM   ◐ 1ST QUARTER

New York City Ballet presents *Contemporary Choreography II* (and May 19, 21, 23, 24).

16 THURSDAY

☼ 5:38 AM / 8:08 PM

Orfeo ed Euridice at the Metropolitan Opera (through Jun. 8)

17 FRIDAY

☼ 5:37 AM / 8:09 PM

An Intimate Evening with David Foster and Katharine McPhee at the St. George Theatre, Staten Island

18 SATURDAY

☼ 5:37 AM / 8:10 PM

Dance Parade and Festival

19 SUNDAY

☼ 5:36 AM / 8:11 PM

AIDS Walk New York, the world's largest and most visible HIV/AIDS fundraising event

May 20–26

"There are the natives, blasé, matter-of-fact, hating the place—unless you say something against it, in which case you have a fist fight on your hands."
—*Esquire*, 1949

20 MONDAY

☼ 5:35 AM / 8:12 PM ♊ GEMINI

The 25th Anniversary OSAKA International Music Competition Gala Concert at Carnegie Hall

21 TUESDAY

☼ 5:34 AM / 8:13 PM

Final chance to see *The Facade Commission: Nairy Baghramian, Scratching the Back* at the Metropolitan Museum of Art

22 WEDNESDAY

☼ 5:33 AM / 8:14 PM

Fleet Week begins (through May 28).

23 THURSDAY

☼ 5:33 AM / 8:15 PM ○ FULL MOON

Vesak

New York Philharmonic presents Mozart's *Requiem*, conducted by Jaap van Zweden (through May 28).

24 FRIDAY

☼ 5:32 AM / 8:15 PM

Evgeny Kissin, piano, at Carnegie Hall (and 29th)

25 SATURDAY

☼ 5:31 AM / 8:16 PM

Bronx Night Market opens for the season at Fordham Plaza (through Oct.).

26 SUNDAY

☼ 5:31 AM / 8:17 PM

New York Youth Symphony at Carnegie Hall

May 27–Jun. 2

"If ever there was an aviary
overstocked with jays, it is that
Yaptown-on-the-Hudson."
  —O. Henry

27 MONDAY

☿ 5:30 AM / 8:18 PM

Memorial Day

Celebrate Memorial Day at Green-
Wood Cemetery's annual concert.

28 TUESDAY

☿ 5:30 AM / 8:19 PM

New York City Ballet presents
A Midsummer Night's Dream (and
May 29, 30, 31, Jun. 1, 2).

29 WEDNESDAY

☿ 5:29 AM / 8:20 PM

2015: One World Observatory opens at
the top of One World Trade Center.

30 THURSDAY

☿ 5:28 AM / 8:20 PM
◑ 3RD QUARTER

1995: NYPD forcefully evicts
squatters who had occupied
abandoned, city-owned buildings
on 13th St. in the Lower East Side.

31 FRIDAY

☿ 5:28 AM / 8:21 PM

South Bronx Culture Festival:
Cumplimos 90. ¡Wepa! (through Jun. 2)

1 SATURDAY

☿ 5:28 AM / 8:22 PM

Brooklyn Film Festival celebrates
its 27th edition at venues in Brooklyn
and online (through Jun. 9).

2 SUNDAY

☿ 5:27 AM / 8:23 PM

University of Texas Wind Ensemble at
Carnegie Hall

JUNE

THE FAMED BIKE MESSENGER of decades past—lean, sinewy, and sweaty, perched on a fixie with a Manhattan Portage bag slung across his chest, and a thick, heavy chain wrapped around his waist, able to down a whole Gatorade in a single gulp—may have faded from memory. These days, a more genteel rider emerges on an electric Dutch cargo bike with kids in tow, or on a pedal-assist Citi Bike in a dress and heels, but fearless riders can still be found on the city streets, from alley-cat road races to the **Harlem Skyscraper Cycling Classic,** a race around Marcus Garvey Park in honor of Father's Day (nicknamed "skinscraper" for its dangerous, tight curves). If sing-alongs are more your thing, find a local **Tony Awards watch party**—like the open-air one in the heart of Times Square. And if you prefer costumes, the **Jazz Age Lawn Party** on Governors Island or the **Mermaid Parade** on Coney Island are the places for you.

PROFESSOR VATICINATE SAYS, *June opens with raindrops on roses, no need for hoses. Sun quickly returns and it turns warm and merry; eat a strawberry. Second week of the month turns sultry and sticky. A dry track for the Belmont Stakes. Mid- to late month remains unseasonably warm; you can hit the beach but keep your umbrella within reach. There'll be lots of "whewmidity."*

NORMALS FOR
CENTRAL PARK
Avg. high: 79.7°
Avg. low: 64.4°
Avg. rainfall: 4.54"

Meteorological summer begins on June 1 and runs until August 31; the warmest three months of the year. Of the top ten warmest summers recorded at Central Park, four have occurred in this century: in 2005, 2010, 2015, and 2016. The warmest summer on record was 2010, with an average temperature of 77.8°. In contrast, the coldest summer was in 1903, which averaged 8° cooler at 69.8°.

SKY WATCH: About an hour before sunrise, the yellow-orange planet Mars hangs low above the eastern horizon. On the morning of the 2nd, Mars will be to the lower left of a crescent Moon; on the following morning Mars will be to the Moon's upper right. The bluish star Spica appears to the right of the gibbous Moon on the 16th. Summer arrives on the 20th at 4:51 p.m. The length of daylight is now at its maximum of fifteen hours and five minutes.

ANNALS OF THE NIGHT SKY

The smallest known star in the universe is EBLM J0555-57Ab, located in the southern constellation of Pictor the Easel. It is comparable in size to the planet Saturn with a diameter of roughly 75,000 miles, but is 250 times more massive. If this star could somehow be reduced to the size of a baseball, our Sun would be a globe measuring over two feet wide.

NYC BOOK OF THE MONTH
Dogfight, A Love Story by Matt Burgess (2010)

This debut novel by Jackson Heights native Matt Burgess unfolds over Father's Day weekend in Queens as Alfredo, a small-time drug dealer, prepares for his brother's return from prison. "Here in Jackson Heights," Burgess writes of his neighborhood, "the parks . . . are asphalt parks, blacktop playgrounds. There aren't any flowers or butterflies, and that keeps exactly nobody away."

NYC MOVIE OF THE MONTH
Die Hard with a Vengeance, directed by John McTiernan, starring Bruce Willis, Samuel L. Jackson, and Jeremy Irons (1995)

NYPD cops (Bruce Willis and Samuel L. Jackson) try to thwart a series of bombings in the highest grossing film of 1995, shot entirely on location from Wall Street to Audubon Avenue. The sweaty pair barrel through a summertime Central Park in a 1987 Chevy Caprice taxi as picnickers jump out of the way. "Are you aiming for these people?" asks Jackson, "No. Well, maybe that mime," retorts Willis.

June has 30 days.

Jun. 3–9

"The only credential the city asked was the boldness to dream."
—Moss Hart

3 MONDAY
☼ 5:27 AM / 8:23 PM

Prima Volta Competition recital at Carnegie Hall

4 TUESDAY
☼ 5:26 AM / 8:24 PM

Last chance to see *Grounded in Clay: The Spirit of Pueblo Pottery* at the Metropolitan Museum of Art

5 WEDNESDAY
☼ 5:26 AM / 8:25 PM

Haskell Small, piano, at Carnegie Hall

6 THURSDAY
☼ 5:26 AM / 8:25 PM ● NEW MOON

D-Day

In his final subscription concert as music director, Jaap van Zweden conducts Mahler's Second Symphony with the New York Philharmonic (through Jun. 8).

7 FRIDAY
☼ 5:26 AM / 8:26 PM

The Belmont Stakes horse race (and 8th)

8 SATURDAY
☼ 5:25 AM / 8:26 PM

Celebrate Ghostbusters Day at Hook and Ladder 8—the firehouse that served as the exterior of Ghostbusters HQ.

9 SUNDAY
☼ 5:25 AM / 8:27 PM

National Puerto Rican Day Parade on 5th Ave.

Tony Awards watch party at Times Square

Jun. 10–16

"At five a.m. Manhattan is a town of tired trumpet players and homeward-bound bartenders. Pigeons control Park Avenue and strut unchallenged in the middle of the street."
—Gay Talese

10 MONDAY
☼ 5:25 AM / 8:28 PM

1936: Staten Island Zoo opens.

11 TUESDAY
☼ 5:25 AM / 8:28 PM

Shavuot begins.

Met Orchestra at Carnegie Hall

12 WEDNESDAY
☼ 5:25 AM / 8:28 PM

City Center Encores! presents *Titanic* (through Jun. 16)

13 THURSDAY
☼ 5:25 AM / 8:29 PM

Shavuot ends.

The Chamber Music Center of New York Concert at Carnegie Hall

14 FRIDAY
☼ 5:25 AM / 8:29 PM   ◐ 1ST QUARTER

Flag Day

Niall Horan: The Show Live on Tour at Madison Square Garden

15 SATURDAY
☼ 5:25 AM / 8:30 PM

Schomburg Literary Festival

16 SUNDAY
☼ 5:25 AM / 8:30 PM

Father's Day

Harlem Skyscraper Cycling Classic around Marcus Garvey Park

● Jun. 17–23

"When it is good, this is a city of fantastic strength, sophistication, and beauty. It is like no other city in time or place."
　—Ada Louise Huxtable

17 MONDAY

☿ 5:25 AM / 8:30 PM

Eid al-Adha

Fresh Start Music Studio Student Recital at Carnegie Hall (and 18th)

18 TUESDAY

☿ 5:25 AM / 8:31 PM

Vision Festival, celebrating free jazz, opens (through Jun. 23).

19 WEDNESDAY

☿ 5:25 AM / 8:31 PM

Juneteenth

Juneteenth Celebration at Carnegie Hall

20 THURSDAY

☿ 5:25 AM / 8:31 PM ♋ CANCER

Summer Solstice

New York International Classic Music Competition at Carnegie Hall

21 FRIDAY

☿ 5:26 AM / 8:31 PM ○ FULL MOON

Viennese Masters Orchestra Invitational at Carnegie Hall

22 SATURDAY

☿ 5:26 AM / 8:32 PM

Coney Island Mermaid Parade and Ball

23 SUNDAY

☿ 5:26 AM / 8:32 PM

1611: Mutineers set Henry Hudson, his son, and loyal crew members adrift in Hudson Bay.

Jun. 24–30

"The outdoors is what you have to pass through to get from your apartment to a taxicab."
—Fran Lebowitz

24 MONDAY

☼ 5:26 AM / 8:32 PM

1965: The Delacorte Music Clock at the Central Park Zoo is dedicated.

25 TUESDAY

☼ 5:27 AM / 8:32 PM

1906: Harry Thaw murders architect Stanford White in a jealous rage over his wife, Evelyn Nesbit.

26 WEDNESDAY

☼ 5:27 AM / 8:32 PM

Celebrate the Cyclone roller coaster's 97th birthday at Luna Park in Coney Island.

27 THURSDAY

☼ 5:27 AM / 8:32 PM

Whitman in Love: "Live Oak, with Moss" and Other Poems in the Garden at the Merchant's House Museum—celebrating Pride Weekend (through Oct. 29)

28 FRIDAY

☼ 5:28 AM / 8:32 PM   ◑ 3RD QUARTER

1969: The Stonewall Uprising starts in the early morning hours.

29 SATURDAY

☼ 5:28 AM / 8:32 PM

The 22nd Annual Rainbows on the Hudson, a Pride Month boat parade organized by the Knickerbocker Sailing Association in support of the Ali Forney Center

30 SUNDAY

☼ 5:29 AM / 8:32 PM

New York City Pride March

JULY

CALL IT LOVE/HATE. Since at least the 1850s, dogs have scurried under beds and children wailed with fear as scofflaws set off fireworks (illegal in the city since 1909) that burst at just the height of a Brooklyn tenement building, or rain sparks from rooftops onto the street. In the 1970s and '80s, mob boss John Gotti provided fireworks for his annual block party in Ozone Park, Queens, while neighbors around Dyckman Street in Inwood still compete for the best show. During the pandemic summer of 2020, no neighborhood was safe from periodic, unexpected explosions. Still, nothing combines New York's spirit of celebration and rebellion, resilience and bravado—and distills the question of who owns the streets—quite like **Independence Day. The Macy's Fourth of July Fireworks show,** best viewed from a Brooklyn rooftop, launches more than 65,000 shells into the sky, reflecting off the shimmery windows of skyscrapers, while the city's parks fill with families enjoying the sticky summer heat.

PROFESSOR VATICINATE SAYS, *surprisingly it's fair and pleasant for Independence Day festivities. But the rest of the month is just plain hot and sticky; we'll all be prisoners of humid bondage. This tropical heat wave will occasionally be broken by skeins of cooling rains.*

NORMALS FOR
CENTRAL PARK

Avg. high: 84.9°
Avg. low: 70.1°
Avg. rainfall: 4.60"

Going back to 1869, there have been sixty days at Central Park when the temperature has reached or topped 100°, and, unsurprisingly, the month that has seen the greatest number of these days (42) is July. In 1966 and 1993, the month had three days when the temperature hit triple digits. In 1936 and 1937, the mercury hit 100° or above back-to-back on the same dates (July 9 and 10). In fact, July 9, 1936, registered the hottest temp ever at Central Park: 106°.

Sky Watch: A stellar eclipse will take place on the 13th, when the Moon crosses in front of the bright blue star Spica, very low in the west-southwest sky. Spica will disappear behind the Moon's dark edge at 11:25 p.m. On the 30th, around 4 a.m., the eastern sky will be adorned with a large triangle composed of a slender crescent Moon, Jupiter, and Mars. And below them will be the orange star Aldebaran.

ANNALS OF THE NIGHT SKY

Fifty years ago, on July 17, 1974, New Yorkers up before sunrise saw the Moon pass in front the planet Venus—this is called an occultation. The *New York Times* featured the headline: "Moon Is a Co-Star With Planet Venus In a Celestial Show." Such a spectacular interaction between two of the brightest objects in the night sky is uncommon. New York City's next opportunity will occur on September 13, 2031.

NYC BOOK OF THE MONTH
A Tree Grows in Brooklyn by Betty Smith (1943)

"Serene was a word you could put to Brooklyn, New York. Especially in the summer of 1912," begins Smith's semi-autobiographical tale of growing up as resilient as the trees—sometimes called "ghetto palms"—that still spring up "in boarded up lots and out of neglected rubbish heaps" in the outer boroughs.

NYC MOVIE OF THE MONTH
The Warriors, directed by Walter Hill, starring Michael Beck, James Remar, and Dorsey Wright (1979)

The Warriors, shot almost entirely on location, tracks a teenage street gang's nighttime journey twenty-seven miles from a "conclave" in the Bronx to home turf on the shores of Coney Island, chased by elaborately costumed rivals who think they've shot a gang leader. Legend has it that real gang members were cast for the conclave scene, with undercover police officers sprinkled in to keep the peace.

July has 31 days.

Jul. 1–7

"Paris is a very graceful and beautiful city, almost too formal and sweet to the taste after the raw disorder of New York."
—Edward Hopper

1 MONDAY
☿ 5:29 AM / 8:32 PM

1972: First issue of *Ms.* magazine is published.

2 TUESDAY
☿ 5:30 AM / 8:32 PM

1939: 200 people attend the first World Science Fiction Convention at Caravan Hall in conjunction with the New York World's Fair.

3 WEDNESDAY
☿ 5:30 AM / 8:31 PM

1937: The front page of the *Daily News* announces Amelia Earhart's plane "Lost at Sea."

4 THURSDAY
☿ 5:31 AM / 8:31 PM

Independence Day

Nathan's Hot Dog Eating Contest at the corner of Stillwell and Surf Aves., Coney Island

5 FRIDAY
☿ 5:31 AM / 8:31 PM ● NEW MOON

1989: *Seinfeld* debuts on NBC.

6 SATURDAY
☿ 5:32 AM / 8:31 PM

Yi-Ling Elaine Lin, soprano, Amy Chiu, piano, and Chia-Min Chen, cello, at Carnegie Hall

7 SUNDAY
☿ 5:33 AM / 8:30 PM

Islamic New Year

Last chance to see *Women's Work* at the New-York Historical Society

Jul. 8–14

"I began to like New York, the racy, adventurous feel of it at night, the satisfaction that the constant flicker of men and women and machines gives to the restless eye."
—F. Scott Fitzgerald

8 MONDAY

☼ 5:33 AM / 8:30 PM

1971: Louis Armstrong lies in state at the 7th Regiment Armory.

9 TUESDAY

☼ 5:34 AM / 8:30 PM

1917: Emma Goldman delivers her "Address to the Jury."

10 WEDNESDAY

☼ 5:35 AM / 8:29 PM

1986: Philippe Petit walks a tightrope across Lincoln Center Plaza.

11 THURSDAY

☼ 5:35 AM / 8:29 PM

1946: Labor leader Sidney Hillman lies in state at Carnegie Hall.

12 FRIDAY

☼ 5:36 AM / 8:28 PM

1976: Madison Square Garden hosts the Democratic National Convention, which nominates Jimmy Carter.

13 SATURDAY

☼ 5:37 AM / 8:28 PM   ◐ 1ST QUARTER

1962: Radio Row business owners protest the plan to raze their neighborhood to construct the World Trade Center.

14 SUNDAY

☼ 5:38 AM / 8:27 PM

Celebrate Bastille Day at a fair on 60th St.

Jul. 15–21

"The city is uncomfortable and inconvenient; but New Yorkers temperamentally do not crave comfort and convenience—if they did they would live elsewhere."
—E. B. White

15 MONDAY

☼ 5:38 AM / 8:27 PM

1938: Welcome parade on Broadway in Lower Manhattan celebrates Howard Hughes's record-breaking global flight.

16 TUESDAY

☼ 5:39 AM / 8:26 PM

1934: Commuter service by seaplane begins from Oyster Bay, Long Island, to Pier 11 at the foot of Wall St.

17 WEDNESDAY

☼ 5:40 AM / 8:25 PM

1950: Julius Rosenberg is arrested on suspicion of espionage.

18 THURSDAY

☼ 5:41 AM / 8:25 PM

1908: The Frogs, an African American theatrical organization, is founded in Harlem.

19 FRIDAY

☼ 5:42 AM / 8:24 PM

2000: Steve Jobs unveils the Power Mac G4 Cube (called "a spectacular failure" by Tim Cook) at Macworld Expo at Javits Center.

20 SATURDAY

☼ 5:42 AM / 8:23 PM

1974: The Ramones decide to make drummer Joey Ramone their lead vocalist.

21 SUNDAY

☼ 5:43 AM / 8:22 PM ○ FULL MOON

1853: New York State legislature sets aside more than 750 acres in the heart of Manhattan to create a landscaped public park—Central Park.

Jul. 22–28

"A crumbling tenement became a secret clubhouse, a rooftop became a private aviary, and a pile of trash might be a source for treasure."
—Martha Cooper

22 MONDAY

☼ 5:44 AM / 8:22 PM ♌ LEO

1849: Emma Lazarus, poet of "The New Colossus," is born in New York.

23 TUESDAY

☼ 5:45 AM / 8:21 PM

1985: At Lincoln Center, Andy Warhol demonstrates the new Amiga computer by digitally manipulating Debby Harry's photo.

24 WEDNESDAY

☼ 5:46 AM / 8:20 PM

1991: Public Enemy plays Radio City Music Hall with Sisters of Mercy.

25 THURSDAY

☼ 5:47 AM / 8:19 PM

1953: The subway token is introduced, and the fare is raised to 15 cents.

26 FRIDAY

☼ 5:48 AM / 8:18 PM

1972: The Rolling Stones play Madison Square Garden on Jagger's 29th birthday—and participate in a pie fight with the audience.

27 SATURDAY

☼ 5:49 AM / 8:17 PM ◑ 3RD QUARTER

1939: East River Park opens—at the time the largest open green space on the Lower East Side.

28 SUNDAY

☼ 5:50 AM / 8:16 PM

1879: Suffragist Lucy Burns is born in Brooklyn.

AUGUST

WHEN SWEAT SEEPS through your button-down shirt, and the sun ricochets off Midtown's office windows and into your eyes, the tree-filled urban oasis of **Washington Square Park**—at ten acres and almost two hundred years old—is a good place to pass an August afternoon and catch a little of the bohemian spirit fostered since 1917, when Ashcan School artists declared "the Free and Independent Republic of Greenwich Village" from atop the square's iconic arch. If you are feeling gutsy you can face off with a park regular in a game of **street chess**—just don't lose your shirt. Gritty, fast-paced, and rowdy, street chess is a hustler's game. If you're feeling even more gutsy, you'll always find **pickup basketball nearby at "the Cage" at West 4th Street,** one of the city's legendary streetball courts. But don't worry, both are also great spectator sports, especially when observed in relative comfort from a distance with an iced coffee or a dipped ice-cream cone or bomb pop from a Mister Softee truck in hand.

PROFESSOR VATICINATE SAYS, *as August opens, a study in pluviography may be useful: for we expect it to be raining cats and dogs, daggers and pitchforks. By the end of the first week, most folks will be asking: "Do you know if that's the Sun or a UFO?" Then, for the rest of the month, the weather will seem like a summer rerun . . . of July! Heat, humidity, and an occasional gully washer. The month ends with a surge of unseasonably chilly air.*

NORMALS FOR CENTRAL PARK
Avg. high: 83.3°
Avg. low: 68.9°
Avg. rainfall: 4.56"

August is the wettest month at Central Park. The wettest August was in 2011, when 18.95" fell—that was the all-time wettest month since recordkeeping began in 1869. The main reason was Tropical Storm Irene on the 28th, which drenched the tristate area with more than six inches of water.

SKY WATCH: This will be an excellent year to watch for the peak of the Perseid meteors, occurring from the 11th to 12th. From a brightly lit city you may catch a few meteors darting from the northeast sky, but from dark, rural locations you may see one every minute or two. Check out the east-northeast sky any time after 1:30 a.m. on the 14th to see an exceedingly close pairing of Jupiter and Mars; Jupiter is nearly sixteen times brighter than its orange companion.

ANNALS OF THE NIGHT SKY

Originally the rule for a Blue Moon—as stated in the now-defunct *Maine Farmers' Almanac*—is that for each season there are usually three full Moons, but sometimes there will be a fourth. In such cases, the third full Moon is designated as a Blue Moon. The 2024 summer season will have four full Moons, so the third (on August 19) may also be considered blue.

NYC BOOK OF THE MONTH
Here is New York by E. B. White (1949)

White tells readers that he penned his classic narrative of the mid-century city "in a stifling hotel room in 90-degree heat, halfway down an air shaft, in midtown . . . twenty-two blocks from where Rudolf Valentino lay in state, eight blocks from where Nathan Hale was executed, five blocks from the publisher's office where Ernest Hemingway hit Max Eastman on the nose." The book encapsulates the layered experience of New York City that persists today.

NYC MOVIE OF THE MONTH
Man on Wire, directed by James Marsh, starring Philippe Petit (2008)

As much a caper film as a documentary, *Man on Wire* combines archival footage with reenactments to tell the tale of "the art crime of the century": the morning of August 7, 1974, when Philippe Petit walked a 200-foot-long tightrope between the towers of the unfinished World Trade Center to the astonishment of the authorities and delight of the crowd watching 1,312 feet below him.

August has 31 days.

Jul. 29–Aug. 4

"The city in summer floated in a daze that moved otherwise sensible people to repeat endlessly the brainless greeting 'Hot enough for ya? Ha-ha.'"
—Arthur Miller

29 MONDAY

☼ 5:51 AM / 8:15 PM

1981: Cheap Trick plays at the Guggenheim at a premiere party for the adult animated film *Heavy Metal*.

30 TUESDAY

☼ 5:52 AM / 8:14 PM

Enjoy an iconic city dessert on National Cheesecake Day.

31 WEDNESDAY

☼ 5:53 AM / 8:13 PM

1979: James Taylor plays Central Park for 250,000 people to raise funds to restore Sheep Meadow.

1 THURSDAY

☼ 5:54 AM / 8:12 PM

1995: The first annual Victoria's Secret Fashion Show at the Plaza Hotel features lots of lingerie, but no wings.

2 FRIDAY

☼ 5:54 AM / 8:11 PM

1964: Jackie Robinson joins a CORE demonstration at the construction site of Downstate Medical Center to protest racial discrimination in hiring.

3 SATURDAY

☼ 5:55 AM / 8:10 PM

1976: Ravi Shankar performs at the Cathedral of Saint John the Divine.

4 SUNDAY

☼ 5:56 AM / 8:09 PM ● NEW MOON

1984: Michael Jackson sings with the Jacksons on the Victory Tour at Madison Square Garden.

Aug. 5–11

"Like basketball, chess hustling is a city game—fast and gritty and played on street corners and in parks with the throb of street life as a backdrop."
    —Dylan Loeb McClain

5 MONDAY
☼ 5:57 AM / 8:08 PM

1937: Ticker tape parade for Douglas "Wrong Way" Corrigan, who flew to Dublin instead of Long Beach, California.

6 TUESDAY
☼ 5:58 AM / 8:07 PM

1885: *Harper's Weekly* depicts a baseball game between the Chicago White Stockings and the New York Giants at the Polo Grounds.

7 WEDNESDAY
☼ 5:59 AM / 8:05 PM

1942: Record producer David Rubinson is born in Brooklyn.

8 THURSDAY
☼ 6:00 AM / 8:04 PM

1987: Billy Idol plays Madison Square Garden.

9 FRIDAY
☼ 6:01 AM / 8:03 PM

1922: Gangster Giuseppe Masseria, "Joe the Boss," survives an assassination attempt that wounds six bystanders and leaves two bullet holes in his straw hat.

10 SATURDAY
☼ 6:02 AM / 8:02 PM

1927: Crowds fill Union Square to protest the impending execution of Nicola Sacco and Bartolomeo Vanzetti.

11 SUNDAY
☼ 6:03 AM / 8:00 PM

Dominican Day Parade, 6th Ave.

Aug. 12–18

"The City is smart at this: smelling and good and looking raunchy."
—Toni Morrison

12 MONDAY

☼ 6:04 AM / 7:59 PM   ◐ 1ST QUARTER

1920: Fans bid farewell to Happy and Fairfax, horses soon to be replaced by a motorized fire truck at Engine Company No. 46.

13 TUESDAY

☼ 6:05 AM / 7:58 PM

1965: Teens (mostly girls) attempt to crash the Warwick Hotel, where the Beatles are staying ahead of their appearance on *The Ed Sullivan Show*.

14 WEDNESDAY

☼ 6:06 AM / 7:56 PM

1993: The Yankees retire Reggie Jackson's number, 44.

15 THURSDAY

☼ 6:07 AM / 7:55 PM

1962: Marvel Comics introduces Spider-Man in issue #15 of *Amazing Fantasy*, written by Stan Lee with illustrations by Steve Ditko.

16 FRIDAY

☼ 6:08 AM / 7:54 PM

Feast of Saint Rocco

1974: The Ramones play CBGB for the first time.

17 SATURDAY

☼ 6:09 AM / 7:52 PM

1807: Robert Fulton's first American steamboat leaves New York City for Albany.

18 SUNDAY

☼ 6:10 AM / 7:51 PM

1969: Christian Slater is born in New York.

Aug. 19–25

"A kind of lazy kinship falls over the city when the heat does and people start talking—out in Washington Square, in the garden of the Museum of Modern Art."
—Joan Didion

---

19 MONDAY

☼ 6:11 AM / 7:49 PM   ○ FULL MOON

1930: Writer Frank McCourt is born in Brooklyn.

---

20 TUESDAY

☼ 6:12 AM / 7:48 PM

1987: Keith Haring paints a mural at Clarkson St. and 7th Ave. in Manhattan.

---

21 WEDNESDAY

☼ 6:13 AM / 7:46 PM

1988: Food truck vendors in City Hall Park protest mayoral regulation that would remove vendors from crowded areas.

---

22 THURSDAY

☼ 6:14 AM / 7:45 PM

♍ VIRGO

1862: Irish American leader of the 69th New York Regiment during the Civil War, General Corcoran, is celebrated at Castle Garden.

---

23 FRIDAY

☼ 6:15 AM / 7:43 PM

1962: Jane Jacobs leads a protest against the proposed Lower Manhattan Expressway.

---

24 SATURDAY

☼ 6:16 AM / 7:42 PM

1962: Mayor Wagner issues a decree defending the right of New Yorkers to purchase a single scoop of ice cream.

---

25 SUNDAY

☼ 6:17 AM / 7:40 PM

1835: The first of six articles of the "Great Moon Hoax" is published in the *New York Sun* newspaper.

Aug. 26–Sep. 1

"I miss New York and its fairy-like
   towers
With Liberty's torch high in the air
I'd give all of California's damn
   flowers
For the sight of Washington Square."
   —Jessie Tarbox Beals, 1936

26 MONDAY

☼ 6:18 AM / 7:39 PM   ◑ 3RD QUARTER

U.S. Open tennis tournament begins
at the Billie Jean King National Tennis
Center in Flushing, Queens.

27 TUESDAY

☼ 6:19 AM / 7:37 PM

Commemorate the Battle of Brooklyn
(1776), the first battle fought after the
signing of the Declaration of Independence, at Green-Wood Cemetery, on
the very land the battle was fought.

28 WEDNESDAY

☼ 6:20 AM / 7:36 PM

1917: Comic book artist Jack Kirby is
born on the Lower East Side.

29 THURSDAY

☼ 6:21 AM / 7:34 PM

1966: Allen Ginsberg reads his poetry
to a crowd in Washington Square Park.

30 FRIDAY

☼ 6:22 AM / 7:33 PM

1962: The second level of the George
Washington Bridge opens, becoming
the world's only fourteen-lane bridge.

31 SATURDAY

☼ 6:23 AM / 7:31 PM

2004: CODEPINK members hold a
"Fox News Shut-Up-A-Thon" in front
of the channel's headquarters during
the Republican Nation Convention,
being held at Madison Square Garden.

1 SUNDAY

☼ 6:24 AM / 7:29 PM

New York Tugboat Race

SEPTEMBER

As BASEBALL SEASON WINDS its way toward the World Series, it's not too late to wind your way through Queens on a Citi Field–bound 7 train to catch a **Mets game.** Sometimes called the "International Express," the 7 train runs through some of the city's most diverse neighborhoods, including Corona, Flushing, and Jackson Heights, where at least 167 languages are spoken, and has spawned "the 7 Line Army" (Mets devotees who consider themselves the largest group of fans in baseball history). Disembark at Junction Boulevard and walk down Roosevelt Avenue for a taste of Queens' street food—such as tamales, elotes, empanadas, and birria tacos—or indulge in craft beer and Shake Shack at the stadium. For a less rowdy time, the **New York City Ballet** and the **Metropolitan Opera** kick off their new seasons, while the **Brooklyn Book Festival** brings bookworms to the borough of Kings.

PROFESSOR VATICINATE SAYS, *unseasonably chilly for Labor Day; too cool for the pool. Expect a protracted spell of dry and chilly weather through midmonth. The second half of September will be quite different: it will be frequently showery and during the third week of the month a hurricane threat may loom along the Atlantic seaboard. Remember: the eye of a hurricane is a void that's wise to avoid.*

NORMALS FOR
CENTRAL PARK
Avg. high: 76.2°
Avg. low: 62.3°
Avg. rainfall: 4.31"

September marks the eightieth anniversary of the Great Atlantic Hurricane of September 15, 1944, which made landfall near Southampton in eastern Long Island with winds of 105 mph. The *New York Times* noted that gale-force winds and torrential rains hit NYC and the metropolitan area, "parts of which reported having taken a beating worse than in the 1938 hurricane."

ANNALS OF THE NIGHT SKY

On the 28th, Comet Tsuchinshan–ATLAS will pass thirty-six million miles from the Sun, and two weeks later will come within forty-four million miles of the Earth. There is a chance that this comet could become bright enough to be readily visible in the west-southwest sky one to three hours after sunset during the third week of October. But a note of caution: comets are notoriously unpredictable. We can only guess how prominent it will become and how long the tail will be. We'll just have to wait and see.

NYC BOOK OF THE MONTH
The House of Mirth by Edith Wharton (1905)

If you stand in Grand Central long enough, you're sure to see someone you know. That's how *The House of Mirth* opens on "a Monday in early September" when, to his surprise, Lawrence Selden's "eyes had been refreshed by the sight of Miss Lily Bart" in the station. The chance encounter leads to an indiscretion—an unchaperoned visit to Selden's apartment—that contributes to the beautiful, but tragically poor, woman's downfall.

NYC MOVIE OF THE MONTH
Desperately Seeking Susan, directed by Susan Seidelman, starring Rosanna Arquette, Madonna, and Aidan Quinn (1985)

Filmed in the late summer and early fall of 1984 at East Village locations from the now-shuttered vintage shop Love Saves the Day to the club Danceteria, *Desperately Seeking Susan* is a movie about amnesia, mistaken identity, and the transformative power of a jacket. In the end, a bored New Jersey housewife (Rosanna Arquette) becomes who she's always wanted to be, someone more like Susan (Madonna, in her first major screen role).

September has 30 days.

Sep. 2–8

"My God, the suburbs! They encircled the city's boundaries like enemy territory and we thought of them as a loss of privacy, a cesspool of conformity, and a life of indescribable dreariness."
—John Cheever

2 MONDAY

☼ 6:25 AM / 7:25 PM   ● NEW MOON

Labor Day

West Indian Carnival (and J'ouvert) in Crown Heights, Brooklyn

3 TUESDAY

☼ 6:26 AM / 7:26 PM

1838: Frederick Douglass embarks on his escape from slavery, heading from Baltimore to New York.

4 WEDNESDAY

☼ 6:27 AM / 7:24 PM

1882: Thomas Edison begins commercial operations at his Pearl St. plant.

5 THURSDAY

☼ 6:28 AM / 7:23 PM

2002: Reopening ceremony for the World Financial Center Winter Garden, after extensive repairs following the September 11 terrorist attack.

6 FRIDAY

☼ 6:29 AM / 7:21 PM

1909: Isaac Zangwill's play *The Melting Pot* opens at the Comedy Theater, popularizing the term.

7 SATURDAY

☼ 6:30 AM / 7:19 PM

1981: President Reagan presents Governor Mario Cuomo and Mayor Ed Koch with an $85 million check for the development of Westway, an unrealized plan to replace the West Side Highway with a buried highway.

8 SUNDAY

☼ 6:31 AM / 7:18 PM

1966: Marc Chagall unveils his murals at the Metropolitan Opera House at Lincoln Center.

Sep. 9–15

"This little low-studded rectangular New York . . . this cramped horizontal gridiron . . . hide-bound in its deadly uniformity of mean ugliness, would fifty years later be as much a vanished city as Atlantis."
—Edith Wharton

9 MONDAY
☼ 6:32 AM / 7:16 PM

1936: Beryl Markham receives the key to the city from Mayor LaGuardia after becoming the first woman to fly across the Atlantic from east to west.

10 TUESDAY
☼ 6:33 AM / 7:14 PM

1919: Nearly a year after the end of World War I, General Pershing is welcomed home with a parade down Fifth Ave. from 107th St. to Washington Square.

11 WEDNESDAY
☼ 6:34 AM / 7:13 PM ☽ 1ST QUARTER

Commemorations of the World Trade Center attack at the 9/11 Memorial

12 THURSDAY
☼ 6:35 AM / 7:11 PM

1960: Hurricane Donna makes landfall in Suffolk County, flooding coastal areas of the city.

13 FRIDAY
☼ 6:36 AM / 7:09 PM

1922: The Straw Hat Riot begins as men protest for the right to wear straw hats beyond September 15.

14 SATURDAY
☼ 6:37 AM / 7:08 PM

1948: Ground breaking for the UN Secretariat Building

15 SUNDAY
☼ 6:38 AM / 7:06 PM

1776: British troops capture Lower Manhattan after landing at what is now Kips Bay on the East River.

Sep. 16–22

"For years New York has shouldered the burden of amusing the rest of the country, which appears to be rather dull."
— A. J. Liebling, 1938

16 MONDAY

☼ 6:39 AM / 7:04 PM

1924: Lauren Bacall is born in the Bronx.

17 TUESDAY

☼ 6:40 AM / 7:03 PM   ○ FULL MOON

1964: UN Secretary-General U Thant unveils Marc Chagall's *Peace Window* at the United Nations.

18 WEDNESDAY

☼ 6:41 AM / 7:01 PM

1968: Mayor Lindsay interviews Barbra Streisand at the premiere of her movie *Funny Girl*.

19 THURSDAY

☼ 6:42 AM / 6:59 PM

Feast of San Gennaro

1969: The Guggenheim Museum opens a solo exhibition of the work of Roy Lichtenstein.

20 FRIDAY

☼ 6:43 AM / 6:57 PM

1979: Pennie Smith photographs Paul Simonon of the Clash smashing his bass guitar at the Palladium—later the cover of *London Calling*.

21 SATURDAY

☼ 6:44 AM / 6:56 PM

German-American Steuben Parade, 5th Ave.

22 SUNDAY

☼ 6:45 AM / 6:54 PM   ♎ LIBRA

Autumnal Equinox

1963: Thousands gather at a rally in NYC to protest the 16th Street Baptist Church bombing in Birmingham, Alabama.

Sep. 23–29

"New York has a trip-hammer vitality which drives you insane with restlessness, if you have no inner stabilizer."
—Henry Miller

23 MONDAY

☼ 6:45 AM / 6:52 PM

1894: Veniero's Pasticceria and Caffè opens at 342 East 11th St. (It's still in business.)

24 TUESDAY

☼ 6:46 AM / 6:51 PM ☽ 3RD QUARTER

1869: The U.S. gold market collapses after President Grant orders the sale of $4 million in government gold to thwart Jay Gould and Jim Fisk's plot to keep the price of gold high.

25 WEDNESDAY

☼ 6:47 AM / 6:49 PM

1952: *Superman* actor Christopher Reeve is born in New York City.

26 THURSDAY

☼ 6:48 AM / 6:47 PM

1909: The International Ladies' Garment Workers Union (Local 25) begins a strike against the Triangle Shirtwaist Company—a year and a half before the infamous fire.

27 FRIDAY

☼ 6:49 AM / 6:45 PM

New York Film Festival (through Oct. 13)

28 SATURDAY

☼ 6:50 AM / 6:44 PM

1966: Marcel Breuer's building for the Whitney Museum opens at 945 Madison Ave. (It's sold to Sotheby's in 2023.)

29 SUNDAY

☼ 6:51 AM / 6:42 PM

1910: Gimbels department store opens its first New York City location at Broadway and 32nd St.

Sep. 30–Oct. 6

"The moon and sun mean nothing to a New Yorker. You can't see the sun out of the subway and you can't see the moon through the top of a taxicab."
—Will Rogers

30 MONDAY

☼ 6:52 AM / 6:40 PM

1920: Miss Grace Lee travels at 100 mph in an open automobile at the Sheepshead Auto Speedway in Brooklyn.

1 TUESDAY

☼ 6:53 AM / 6:39 PM

1962: Johnny Carson takes over as host of NBC's *Tonight Show*, with Groucho Marx as his first guest.

2 WEDNESDAY

☼ 6:54 AM / 6:37 PM ● NEW MOON

Rosh Hashana begins.

1945: Sixth Avenue is formally named Avenue of the Americas to express "love and affection . . . for our sister republics of Central and South America," according to Mayor LaGuardia.

3 THURSDAY

☼ 6:55 AM / 6:35 PM

1941: *The Maltese Falcon* premieres in New York City.

4 FRIDAY

☼ 6:56 AM / 6:34 PM

Rosh Hashana ends.

1965: Pope Paul VI holds mass at Yankee Stadium during a fourteen-hour visit to New York City.

5 SATURDAY

☼ 6:58 AM / 6:32 PM

Brooklyn Book Festival Children's Day in Downtown Brooklyn

6 SUNDAY

☼ 6:59 AM / 6:30 PM

Brooklyn Book Festival in Downtown Brooklyn

OCTOBER

First organized in 1974 by puppeteer and artist Ralph Lee, the **Greenwich Village Halloween Parade** is still known for its elaborate, handmade puppets, but any costumed New Yorker can join 60,000 of their friends as the parade steps off at Canal Street and Sixth Avenue. Chaos reigns in the West Village as parade goers fill the surrounding streets and bars for a night of partying. But for delight, indulgence, and sheer cuteness, head to Tompkins Square Park for the **Halloween Dog Parade** or Brooklyn's Fort Greene Park for their **Great PUPkin Dog Costume Contest**; where else can you find a Pomeranian dressed as King Tut, or a corgi dressed as a Chia Pet? Honor Italian heritage at the **Columbus Day Parade** or celebrate the resilience of New York's first peoples with the **Indigenous Peoples' Day** festival on Randall's Island with drumming, singing, and dancing. Don't forget to catch the best in world cinema at the **New York Film Festival** presented by Film at Lincoln Center.

Professor Vaticinate says, *October will initially live up to its title as the clearest month of the year. The first week of the month will feature dry and cool days; bright and cheery, dearie. But sorry my dear, October can't all be clear: week two sees a nor'easter at least, or rain, that's plain. Third week turns blustery and chilly; bright, but button up tight! Unsettled weather arrives in time for Halloween. Could be more of a trick than a treat.*

Normals for Central Park

Avg. high: 64.5°
Avg. low: 51.4°
Avg. rainfall: 4.38"
Avg. snowfall: 0.1"

October marks the seventieth anniversary of Hurricane Hazel, whose remnants passed through central Pennsylvania on the evening of October 15, 1954. Not much rain fell in the City, but the winds were fierce, with a peak gust of 113 mph recorded at the Battery at the south end of Manhattan; the Empire State Building swayed slightly.

October is the clearest month: 12 days average less than 3/10 cloud cover.

SKY WATCH: Shortly after sunset on the 5th, Venus will sit to the upper right of a slender crescent Moon. During the overnight hours of the 16th–17th, the full Moon will coincide with perigee, its closest point to Earth. On such occasions, the Moon appears 7 percent larger and 15 percent brighter than average. The mainstream media refers to this as a "supermoon."

ANNALS OF THE NIGHT SKY

The movie *Frequency* (2000) features an unusually intense display of the aurora borealis over NYC, coinciding with the 1969 World Series. Interestingly, a spectacular display of the northern lights did occur in 1969, but not in October. On the evening of Sunday, March 23, a brilliant aurora was seen as far south as Texas. At New York's Jones Beach, four hundred people who gathered for a star party witnessed "waves of pulsating light" tinged in green, white, and crimson.

NYC BOOK OF THE MONTH
Brown Girl, Brownstones by Paule Marshall (1959)

Set in Brooklyn's Bedford-Stuyvesant, Marshall drew on her own Brooklyn upbringing as the daughter of immigrants in this novel about an upwardly mobile family from Barbados. Torn between the mother's wish to purchase the brownstone they rent, and the father's desire to return to their homeland, a daughter seeks to find herself.

NYC MOVIE OF THE MONTH
Ghostbusters, directed by Ivan Reitman, starring Bill Murray, Dan Aykroyd, Harold Ramis, Rick Moranis, and Sigourney Weaver (1984)

Partially filmed on location in New York City—from guerilla shots at Rockefeller Center to a rush-hour shutdown of streets around 55 Central Park West, which blocked traffic all the way to Brooklyn—this tale of ghost-hunting hijinks by a band of unlikely heroes culminates with a flaming Stay Puft Marshmallow Man wreaking King Kong–like havoc on Columbus Circle.

October has 31 days.

Oct. 7–13

"It is still true that if you scratch an old New Yorker, you find a Victorian."

—New Yorker, 1926

7 MONDAY

☼ 7:00 AM / 6:29 PM

Curbside composting begins in Manhattan.

8 TUESDAY

☼ 7:01 AM / 6:27 PM

1941: Weegee photographs *Their First Murder*, a shot of mostly schoolchildren at the scene of gambler Peter Mancuso's murder in Williamsburg.

9 WEDNESDAY

☼ 7:02 AM / 6:26 PM

1957: The *Daily News* cover story reports, "Dodgers Go To L.A. Next Year: Move Ends NL Ball in NY."

10 THURSDAY

☼ 7:03 AM / 6:24 PM ◑ 1ST QUARTER

1990: ACT UP holds a Clean Needles for AIDS Prevention march in Foley Square.

11 FRIDAY

☼ 7:04 AM / 6:22 PM

1884: Eleanor Roosevelt is born in Manhattan.

12 SATURDAY

☼ 7:05 AM / 6:21 PM

Yom Kippur

Pumpkin picking at Historic Richmond Town's Decker Farm (Sat. and Sun. through Oct.)

13 SUNDAY

☼ 7:06 AM / 6:19 PM

1962: Edward Albee's *Who's Afraid of Virginia Woolf?* opens on Broadway at the Billy Rose Theatre.

Oct. 14–20

"This city is reward for all it will enable you to achieve and punishment for all the crimes it will force you to commit."
—Colson Whitehead

14 MONDAY

☼ 7:07 AM / 6:18 PM

Indigenous People's Day · Columbus Day

Indigenous People's Day celebrations at the National Museum of the American Indian

Columbus Day Parade on Fifth Ave.

15 TUESDAY

☼ 7:08 AM / 6:16 PM

1969: Protesters fill Bryant Park for the Moratorium to End the War in Vietnam, a nationwide protest.

16 WEDNESDAY

☼ 7:09 AM / 6:15 PM

Sukkot begins.

1916: Margaret Sanger opens her first birth control clinic in Brooklyn.

17 THURSDAY

☼ 7:10 AM / 6:13 PM
○ FULL MOON

1957: Producer Mike Todd throws a party for himself with 18,000 "close friends" at Madison Square Garden—including a fourteen-foot-high cake and 25,000 hot dogs—that quickly turns into a food fight.

18 FRIDAY

☼ 7:11 AM / 6:12 PM

Open House New York Weekend (through Oct. 20)

19 SATURDAY

☼ 7:12 AM / 6:10 PM

1962: Judson Memorial Church screens the film adaptation of Jack Gelber's *The Connection* in defiance of the New York State Board of Regent's refusal to approve it for public movie houses.

20 SUNDAY

☼ 7:14 AM / 6:09 PM

1979: Feminists stage an antipornography march in Times Square.

Oct. 21–27

"Comparing the Brooklyn that I know with Manhattan is like comparing a comfortable and complacent duenna to her more brilliant and neurotic sister."
—Carson McCullers

21 MONDAY

☼ 7:15 AM / 6:07 PM

1957: Queen Elizabeth II has a ticker tape parade, visits the Empire State Building, and gives a speech at the UN General Assembly.

22 TUESDAY

☼ 7:16 AM / 6:06 PM ♏ SCORPIO

1903: Curly Howard, of the Three Stooges, is born in Bensonhurst, Brooklyn.

23 WEDNESDAY

☼ 7:17 AM / 6:05 PM

Sukkot ends.

1915: More than 25,000 women march up Fifth Ave. to advocate for women's suffrage.

24 THURSDAY

☼ 7:18 AM / 6:03 PM ☽ 3RD QUARTER

Candlelight Ghost Tour at the Merchant's House Museum (and Oct. 25, 26, 31)

25 FRIDAY

☼ 7:19 AM / 6:02 PM

1957: Albert Anastasia, mobster and cofounder of Murder, Inc., is murdered in a barber's chair at the Park Sheraton Hotel.

26 SATURDAY

☼ 7:20 AM / 6:01 PM

1993: Björk films the video for "Big Time Sensuality" on the back of a truck driving through New York City.

27 SUNDAY

☼ 7:22 AM / 5:59 PM

1925: Steinway Hall on West 57th St. holds its grand opening concert.

Oct. 28–Nov. 3

"New York has total depth in every area. Washington has only politics; after that, the second biggest thing is white marble."
—John Lindsay

28 MONDAY
☼ 7:23 AM / 5:58 PM

1961: Shea Stadium ground breaking

29 TUESDAY
☼ 7:24 AM / 5:57 PM

1859: Charles Ebbets, co-owner of the Brooklyn Dodgers, is born in Greenwich Village.

30 WEDNESDAY
☼ 7:25 AM / 5:55 PM

2000: After beating the Mets in the first Subway Series in forty-four years, the Yankees are given a ticker tape parade.

31 THURSDAY
☼ 7:26 AM / 5:54 PM

Halloween

Greenwich Village Halloween Parade

1 FRIDAY
☼ 7:27 AM / 5:53 PM ● NEW MOON

Diwali/Deepavali

1994: Nirvana releases their *MTV Unplugged in New York* album.

2 SATURDAY
☼ 7:29 AM / 5:52 PM

1913: Actor Burt Lancaster is born on 106th St. in Manhattan.

3 SUNDAY
☼ 6:30 AM / 4:51 PM

Daylight saving time ends.

New York City Marathon

NOVEMBER

NEW YORKERS WALK FAST, and talk faster, but the fastest New Yorkers lace up their running shoes for the **Marathon.** In the time it takes most of us to walk over a few Upper East Side avenues, the elite runners have already been to the Bronx and back. The party atmosphere along the parade route, as neighbors line up from Brooklyn to the Bronx to cheer on friends and strangers alike, makes it easy to forget that winter's chill is on the way. It's hard to admit, but early November is also a great time to escape the boroughs for **leaf peeping** along the Hudson River—just hop on Metro-North's Hudson Line for a day trip to Beacon or Cold Spring. If nature's not your thing, the **New York Comedy Festival** brings two hundred comedians to venues in all five boroughs. At the end of the month, avoid **Black Friday's shopping** crush as crowds bulge off the sidewalks and onto the streets on Fifth Avenue in Midtown or Broadway in SoHo. New Yorkers know the best shopping is done midweek at lunchtime.

PROFESSOR VATICINATE SAYS, *dry and chilly conditions favor marathon participants. Then, roll up your sleeves and rake some leaves. Mellow yellow, then during the second and third weeks of the month, rain (and maybe even some flakes of wet snow) makes you bellow. Last, but certainly not least, the weather goes from dismal to abysmal by Thanksgiving time with a possible coastal storm.*

NORMALS FOR
CENTRAL PARK

Avg. high: 54.0°
Avg. low: 42.0°
Avg. rainfall: 3.58"
Avg. snowfall: 0.5"

Since we are voting for the president this year, here are weather extremes that have occurred in NYC for past presidential election years. The warmest was 75° on November 3, 1936 (Roosevelt). The coldest was 30° on November 8, 1960 (Kennedy), and the wettest saw 2.18" of rain on November 3, 1992 (Clinton). Snow has never fallen on a presidential election day, though in 2012 it snowed 4.3" on the following day.

SKY WATCH: On the 10th at 10 p.m., you'll see Saturn hovering very close to the Moon's upper right. For the second time this year, the Moon will occult (hide) the bright blue star Spica during the morning hours of the 27th. The Moon will be a slender crescent in the lower southeast when Spica disappears at 5:37 a.m. Reappearance comes at 6:51 a.m., but sunrise comes only five minutes later.

ANNALS OF THE NIGHT SKY

Although it's the second-largest planet in the solar system, Saturn is mostly made up of gas, which is less dense than water. So, if you could find a bathtub big enough to drop Saturn into, it would float!

NYC BOOK OF THE MONTH
Behold the Dreamers by Imbolo Mbue (2016)

Mbue's debut novel charts the impact of the 2008 financial crisis through the stories of two intertwined families. Jende Jonga supports his immigrant family as a chauffeur for Lehman executive Clark Edwards—a job he gets in the fall of 2007. Jonga is struck by "the thousand autumn-drenched trees and proud towers of Manhattan" outside the windows of Edwards's office, "the likes of which he'd never seen."

NYC MOVIE OF THE MONTH
She's Gotta Have It, directed by Spike Lee, starring
Tracy Camilla Johns, Tommy Redmond Hicks,
John Canada Terrell, and Spike Lee (1986)

Free-spirited Brooklyn artist Nola Darling cooks her first Thanksgiving dinner for all three of her lovers in Spike Lee's exploration of liberated female sexuality. Lee's first feature-length film, shot over twelve days in and around Fort Greene, is a classic of independent cinema and a tribute to the vibrant life of Lee's own neighborhood.

November has 30 days.

Nov. 4–10

"New York is large, glamorous, easy-going, kindly, and incurious—but above all it is a crucible."
—Ford Madox Ford

4 MONDAY
☼ 6:31 AM / 4:49 PM

New York Comedy Festival
(through Nov. 10)

5 TUESDAY
☼ 6:32 AM / 4:48 PM

Election Day

1941: Art Garfunkel is born in Forest Hills, Queens.

6 WEDNESDAY
☼ 6:33 AM / 4:47 PM

1965: Activist Dorothy Day gives a speech during an antidraft demonstration at Union Square as men burn their draft cards.

7 THURSDAY
☼ 6:35 AM / 4:46 PM

1985: *After Tilted Arc*, curated by Tom Finkelpearl, opens at the Storefront for Art and Architecture.

8 FRIDAY
☼ 6:36 AM / 4:45 PM

1899: Bronx Zoological Gardens opens to the public with 843 animals.

9 SATURDAY
☼ 6:37 AM / 4:44 PM ◑ IST QUARTER

1965: A massive blackout traps more than 800,000 riders in the city's subways.

10 SUNDAY
☼ 6:38 AM / 4:43 PM

2009: U.S. Marshals Service previews 400 pieces of jewelry and antiques seized from Bernie Madoff that are set to go to auction.

Nov. 11–17

"When you give up your apartment in New York and move to another city, New York becomes the worst version of itself. . . . It's much more expensive . . . and much more unfriendly."
—Nora Ephron

---

11 MONDAY

☼ 6:39 AM / 4:42 PM

Veterans Day

1818: James Renwick Jr., architect of Saint Patrick's Cathedral, is born in New York.

---

12 TUESDAY

☼ 6:41 AM / 4:41 PM

1995: The "Five Boroughs" subway token—with its pentagram-shaped hole—debuts with a $1.50 fare.

---

13 WEDNESDAY

☼ 6:42 AM / 4:40 PM

1980: Martin Scorsese's *Raging Bull* with Robert De Niro and Joe Pesci premieres in New York.

---

14 THURSDAY

☼ 6:43 AM / 4:40 PM

1889: Journalist Nellie Bly sets off on her round-the-world trip for the *New York World*.

---

15 FRIDAY

☼ 6:44 AM / 4:39 PM   ○ FULL MOON

1977: Devo records *Live at Max's Kansas City*.

---

16 SATURDAY

☼ 6:45 AM / 4:38 PM

1983: Hall & Oates shoot the video for "Say It Isn't So" at the West 23rd St. pier.

---

17 SUNDAY

☼ 6:47 AM / 4:37 PM

1962: The *New Yorker* publishes "Letter from a Region in My Mind," by James Baldwin.

Nov. 18–24

"I get out of the taxi and it's probably the only city which in reality looks better than on the postcards, New York."

—Milos Forman

18 MONDAY

☿ 6:47 AM / 4:36 PM

1985: Def Jam Recordings releases its first full-length album, LL Cool J's *Radio*.

19 TUESDAY

☿ 6:49 AM / 4:36 PM

2003: Eight finalists for the World Trade Center Memorial are displayed at the Winter Garden.

20 WEDNESDAY

☿ 6:50 AM / 4:35 PM

1929: *The Rise of the Goldbergs*, a radio program about a Jewish family in the Bronx, premieres—it would later become a TV show running from 1949 to 1956.

21 THURSDAY

☿ 6:51 AM / 4:34 PM ♐ SAGITTARIUS

1834: Hetty Green, the "Witch of Wall Street," is born in New Bedford, MA.

22 FRIDAY

☿ 6:52 AM / 4:34 PM ☽ 3RD QUARTER

1913: *Harper's Weekly* publishes the first chapters of Louis Brandeis's *Other People's Money and How the Bankers Use It*.

23 SATURDAY

☿ 6:53 AM / 4:33 PM

1943: Weegee snaps a photograph of Mrs. George Washington Kavanaugh and Lady Decies on the way to the Metropolitan Opera, while a homeless woman stands nearby.

24 SUNDAY

☿ 6:55 AM / 4:33 PM

1972: Lou Reed's "Walk on the Wild Side" is released.

Nov. 25–Dec. 1

"The true New Yorker secretly believes that people living anywhere else have to be, in some sense, kidding."
—John Updike

25 MONDAY

☼ 6:56 AM / 4:32 PM

1783: General George Washington rides into New York City with 800 soldiers as the British evacuate.

26 TUESDAY

☼ 6:57 AM / 4:32 PM

1963: The *Daily News* prints a cover photo of John F. Kennedy Jr. saluting his father's casket.

27 WEDNESDAY

☼ 6:58 AM / 4:31 PM

1924: The *Times* reports "a retinue of clowns, freaks, animals, and floats" at the first Macy's Thanksgiving Day Parade.

28 THURSDAY

☼ 6:59 AM / 4:31 PM

Thanksgiving Day

Macy's Thanksgiving Day Parade

29 FRIDAY

☼ 7:00 AM / 4:31 PM

Native American Heritage Day

A Christmas Carol at the Merchant's House: *Charles Dickens in New York, 1867* in the museum's grand double parlor (through Dec. 29)

30 SATURDAY

☼ 7:01 AM / 4:30 PM

1924: Shirley Chisholm, the first African American woman in Congress, is born in Brooklyn.

1 SUNDAY

☼ 7:02 AM / 4:30 PM   ● NEW MOON

1962: Robert Moses announces he will quit his five New York State government posts, following a dispute with Governor Rockefeller.

DECEMBER

THE HOLIDAY SEASON commences with the fragrance of pine needles competing with the gooey sweetness of roasted nuts, steaming in the cold December air. Firs, spruces, and pines sprout overnight on sidewalks from Brooklyn to the Bronx. The charming demeanor of the Christmas tree vendor—part carnival barker, part salesman, sometimes with a French Canadian accent—masks cold, long hours and cutthroat competition for the best stands. It can be romantic, if impractical, to **shop for the perfect tree** in the snow (think *When Harry Met Sally*). But if dragging a cold, wet tree up five flights of stairs as it rains needles onto the stairway (which, despite your best sweeping efforts, will still be there in June) changes the mood, head to **Dyker Heights for New York's best neighborhood Christmas lights spectacle,** or grab a gift and a hot chocolate or a hot apple cider at one of the many **holiday markets** that pop up from Union Square to Bryant Park.

PROFESSOR VATICINATE SAYS, *during December's first week, batten down for yet another coastal storm; a brief spell of balmy and mild turns to bleak and wild. For much of this twelfth month in fact, we'll endure "3D weather": dull, dank, and dreary. Not necessarily a white Christmas, but perhaps a white New Year? Turning blustery and colder with flurries. Now with mittens on, we'll wave, so long!*

NORMALS FOR
CENTRAL PARK

Avg. high: 44.3°
Avg. low: 33.8°
Avg. rainfall: 4.38"
Avg. snowfall: 4.9"

NYC in the 1970s and 1980s saw few heavy snowfalls. In fact, only six times in the '70s and five times in the '80s were there winters when snowstorms of 6" or more took place. But in the 1990s, eleven storms of a half-foot or more occurred. That number rose to thirteen in the 2000s and eighteen in the 2010s, which also saw three storms that dumped 20" or more, including an unheard-of two in one year (February 25–27 and December 26–27, 2010).

SKY WATCH: After sunset on the 4th, enjoy the pleasing celestial tableau of dazzling Venus sitting to the upper right of a crescent Moon. A nearly full Moon will ruin this year's Geminid meteor shower on the night of the 13th–14th, hiding most of the fainter meteors, although an outstandingly bright Geminid fireball can still attract attention even in moonlight. Winter officially arrives on the 21st at 4:20 a.m.

ANNALS OF THE NIGHT SKY

Fifty years ago, on December 13 (a Friday), two New York–based astronomy clubs gathered on the eighty-sixth floor observation deck of the Empire State Building to observe a partial eclipse of the Sun. Unfortunately, cloudy skies hid the entire event. One radio reporter who was present later noted: "It was the biggest cover-up since Watergate."

NYC BOOK OF THE MONTH
The Price of Salt by Patricia Highsmith (1952)

Highsmith was inspired to write this novel of forbidden romance between two women while working as a holiday salesclerk at Bloomingdales, where she encountered an elegant "blondish woman in a fur coat" who purchased a doll—a scene she wrote into the book. Released the same year that homosexuality was classified as a mental illness, the book hints—radically—at a happy ending for the lovers. It was later adapted as the movie *Carol* (2015).

NYC MOVIE OF THE MONTH
The French Connection, directed by William Friedkin, starring Gene Hackman, Roy Scheider, and Fernando Rey (1971)

This neo-noir is best known for an epic car chase in which a cop in a civilian Pontiac pursues a hit man on a hijacked elevated train (the BMT in Bensonhurst, Brooklyn). Friedkin claims he bribed a transit official for the train, and taunted stunt driver Bill Hickman to drive twenty-six blocks at ninety mph without a permit or even blocking traffic. In another scene, a cop dressed in a Santa suit chases a suspect through garbage-strewn lots—a detail inspired by the tactics of real-life undercover officer Edward Egan.

December has 31 days.

Dec. 2–8

"It was just dusk and it looked as if the buildings were a great dark mountain and the lights looked like gems among them."
—Naomi R. King, 1899

2 MONDAY
☼ 7:03 AM / 4:30 PM

1939: Mayor LaGuardia presides over the opening of the airport that now bears his name.

3 TUESDAY
☼ 7:04 AM / 4:30 PM

1984: Roy Lichtenstein's *Greene Street Mural* is exhibited at Leo Castelli Gallery.

4 WEDNESDAY
☼ 7:05 AM / 4:29 PM

Rockefeller Center Christmas Tree Lighting

5 THURSDAY
☼ 7:06 AM / 4:29 PM

1905: Mark Twain celebrates his seventieth birthday at Delmonico's with 170 guests.

6 FRIDAY
☼ 7:07 AM / 4:29 PM

1962: Andy Warhol's first solo exhibition opens at Stable Gallery.

7 SATURDAY
☼ 7:08 AM / 4:29 PM

Pearl Harbor Remembrance Day

1767: The John Street Theatre—the city's first—opens at 15–21 John St.

8 SUNDAY
☼ 7:09 AM / 4:29 PM   ☽ 1ST QUARTER

1941: New York City puts all 116,000 air raid wardens on alert following the United States' declaration of war on Japan.

Dec. 9–15

"I believe in New Yorkers. Whether they've ever questioned the dream in which they live, I wouldn't know, because I won't ever dare ask that question."
—Dylan Thomas

9 MONDAY
☿ 7:10 AM / 4:29 PM

2002: *The Gangs of New York* premieres at the Ziegfeld Theater.

10 TUESDAY
☿ 7:10 AM / 4:29 PM

1973: CBGB opens in New York City.

11 WEDNESDAY
☿ 7:11 AM / 4:29 PM

1882: Fiorello LaGuardia is born in Greenwich Village.

12 THURSDAY
☿ 7:12 AM / 4:29 PM

1745: John Jay, second governor of New York and first chief justice of the United States, is born in NYC.

13 FRIDAY
☿ 7:13 AM / 4:30 PM

1986: Activist and organizer Ella Baker dies in Manhattan.

14 SATURDAY
☿ 7:13 AM / 4:30 PM

1978: Billy Joel plays Madison Square Garden for the first time.

15 SUNDAY
☿ 7:14 AM / 4:30 PM   ○ FULL MOON

The annual Clement Clarke Moore Memorial Candlelight Service at Church of the Intercession, where the author is buried.

Dec. 16–22

"Chicago is the great American city. New York is one of the capitals of the world and Los Angeles is a constellation of plastic."
—Norman Mailer

16 MONDAY

☼ 7:15 AM / 4:30 PM

1912: Women's Suffrage Hike organized by Rosalie Gardiner Jones marches from the Bronx to Albany.

17 TUESDAY

☼ 7:15 AM / 4:31 PM

1971: John Lennon, Yoko Ono, and Aretha Franklin perform at a benefit at the Apollo for Attica Prison Uprising families.

18 WEDNESDAY

☼ 7:16 AM / 4:31 PM

1952: Ticker tape parade for Lt. Gen. Willis D. Crittenberger, retiring commander of the First Army.

19 THURSDAY

☼ 7:17 AM / 4:31 PM

1918: Ripley's "Believe it or Not!" is published for the first time in the *New York Globe*.

20 FRIDAY

☼ 7:17 AM / 4:32 PM

1993: Donald Trump marries Marla Maples at the Plaza Hotel.

21 SATURDAY

☼ 7:18 AM / 4:32 PM ♑ CAPRICORN

Winter Solstice

1965: The first helicopter service between JFK and the new Pan Am Building takes off amid protests from Tudor City residents like Katharine Hepburn.

22 SUNDAY

☼ 7:18 AM / 4:33 PM ☽ 3RD QUARTER

1966: Julie Nixon (daughter of the president) marries David Eisenhower (grandson of the president) at Marble Collegiate Church.

Dec. 23–29

"New York dresses up at Christmas. It becomes a beautiful dream who wears her spangles and dangerous charm gaily and sweetly . . . she is the most irresistible siren in the world."

—*Esquire*, 1949

23 MONDAY

☼ 7:18 AM / 4:33 PM

1944: Charles Dana Gibson, creator of the Gibson Girl, dies in Manhattan.

24 TUESDAY

☼ 7:19 AM / 4:34 PM

Christmas Eve

1927: Novelist Mary Higgins Clark is born in the Bronx.

25 WEDNESDAY

☼ 7:19 AM / 4:35 PM

Christmas Day

Hanukkah begins.

Eat at a Chinese restaurant.

26 THURSDAY

☼ 7:20 AM / 4:35 PM

Kwanzaa begins.

1965: Duke Ellington performs one of three Sacred Concerts with Lena Horn at the Fifth Avenue Presbyterian Church.

27 FRIDAY

☼ 7:20 AM / 4:36 PM

1932: Radio City Music Hall opens.

28 SATURDAY

☼ 7:20 AM / 4:36 PM

1922: Comic book creator Stan Lee is born on West 98th St. in Manhattan.

29 SUNDAY

☼ 7:20 AM / 4:37 PM

1936: Mary Tyler Moore is born in Brooklyn.

Dec. 30–Jan. 5

"The two moments when New York seems most desirable . . . are just as you are leaving and must say good-bye, and just as you return and can say hello."
—*New Yorker*, 1955

30 MONDAY

☼ 7:21 AM / 4:38 PM ● NEW MOON

1956: The New York Giants beat the Chicago Bears in the NFL championship game at Yankee Stadium (and wait thirty years before their next win).

31 TUESDAY

☼ 7:21 AM / 4:39 PM

New Year's Eve

Times Square Ball Drop

NYRR Midnight Run (a party all of its own)

I WEDNESDAY

☼ 7:20 AM / 4:40 PM

New Year's Day

Kwanzaa ends.

2 THURSDAY

☼ 7:20 AM / 4:41 PM

Hanukkah ends.

1965: The New York Jets sign Joe Namath for $427,000 over three years—a pro football record.

3 FRIDAY

☼ 7:20 AM / 4:42 PM

1920: The Boston Red Sox announce an agreement to sell Babe Ruth to the Yankees—starting the 84-year "Curse of the Bambino."

4 SATURDAY

☼ 7:20 AM / 4:43 PM

1865: The New York Stock Exchange opens its first permanent headquarters on Broad Street.

5 SUNDAY

☼ 7:20 AM / 4:44 PM

1950: Chris Stein, of Blondie, is born in Brooklyn.

The Sun Will Darken On April 8

MARK MONDAY, APRIL 8, on your calendar as "Solar Eclipse Day," for if the weather is fair, you should have no difficulty observing a large partial eclipse of the Sun from New York City. Other areas will experience a *total* eclipse, in which the Moon completely blocks out the disk of the Sun. During a total eclipse, we are treated to a rare view of the Sun's pearly corona; a remarkable sight. At the same time, darkness settles over the landscape, allowing some of the brighter stars and planets to be seen. Meanwhile, an eerie saffron glow rims the horizon.

The path of totality, averaging 123 miles wide, runs from southwest Texas to northern New England. Cities within the totality zone include San Antonio, Austin, Dallas–Fort Worth, Little Rock, Cape Girardeau, Indianapolis, Cleveland, Erie, Buffalo, Rochester, Syracuse, Burlington, and Presque Isle. The duration of totality will vary from nearly 4½ minutes in Texas to over 3¼ minutes in Maine.

Unfortunately, New York City will not experience the total eclipse, but as a consolation prize, the city will see the passing New Moon cover a large fraction of the Sun; an unearthly twilight will fall as the Sun is reduced to a slender crescent. At 3:25 p.m. EDT, 90 percent of the Sun's disk will be obscured—the maximum coverage for the Big Apple.

The eclipse will begin at 2:10 p.m. and end at 4:36 p.m., when the Moon moves clear of the Sun. Warning is usually given at eclipse times against looking at the Sun with bare eyes, as blindness could ensue. This has given some people the idea that eclipses are dangerous. Not so!

It's the *Sun* that's dangerous. All the time!

There are safe ways to gaze at the Sun, however. For details on safely viewing the eclipse, visit the American Astronomical Society's authoritative site: **eclipse.aas.org/eye-safety**.

To all of you planning to watch, especially from the totality zone, good luck and clear skies!

"The Sun may be in eclipse, but New York, never!"
—Mayor John F. Hylan, quoted during a total
solar eclipse over NYC, January 24, 1925